THE COMPLETE
ROUTE 66
LOST & FOUND

RUSSELL A. OLSEN

This edition first published in 2008 by Voyageur Press, an imprint of MBI Publishing Company, 400 First Avenue North, Suite 300, Minneapolis, MN 55401 USA

Voyageur Press titles are also available at discounts in bulk quantity for industrial or sales-promotional use. For details write to Special Sales Manager at MBI Publishing Company, 400 First Avenue North, Suite 300, Minneapolis, MN 55401 USA.

To find out more about our books, join us online at www.voyageurpress.com.

Library of Congress Cataloging-in-Publication Data

Olsen, Russell A., 1954-
  [Route 66, lost & found]
  The complete Route 66 lost & found / by Russell A. Olsen.
       p. cm.
  Originally published in 2 v. under titles: Route 66, lost & found and Route 66, lost & found. v.2, 2004–2006.
  Includes bibliographical references and index.
  ISBN 978-0-7603-3492-8 (plc)
  1. West (U.S.)—Pictorial works. 2. United States Highway 66—Pictorial works. 3.   Roadside architecture—West (U.S.)—Pictorial works. 4. Historic sites—West (U.S.)—Pictorial works. 5. Postcards—West (U.S.) 6. West (U.S.)—Description and travel. 7. Olsen, Russell, A., 1954—Travel—West (U.S.) I. Title. II. Title: Complete Route 66 lost and found.
  F590.7.O53 2008
  978'.0330222—dc22

                                                   2008007294

About the Author: Russell Olsen began exploring and photographing Route 66 in 1995. On his first trip down The Mother Road he unexpectedly shot 27 rolls of film. Annual trips followed and in 1998 Olsen set out on his "Lost & Found" project, collecting vintage postcards, photographing Route 66 and publishing the first volume of *Route 66 Lost & Found* in 2004, and the second volume in 2006. Born and raised in South Chicago, Olsen today lives in North Hollywood, California. His work can be viewed at www.route66lostandfound.com.

Printed in China

CONTENTS

CONTENTS

ROUTE 66
LOST & FOUND
RUINS AND RELICS REVISITED

RUSSELL A. OLSEN

Voyageur Press

PREFACE AND ACKNOWLEDGMENTS

In late summer 1995, I drove to Chicago from Los Angeles to visit my brother and his family. While there, I had the thought to drive Route 66 back west. I had always wanted to take this trip, and it seemed like the perfect opportunity to cross one of the items off my "things to accomplish in my life" list. So I borrowed a camera from my brother and bought a couple rolls of film on which to record my much-anticipated trip. I soon realized that two rolls of film were not going to cut it. I found a wealth of subject matter and wound up shooting 27 rolls of film on that trip.

That was the beginning of my fascination with America's Main Street. During the next few years I made the trip from Los Angeles to Chicago on an annual basis, spending most of my time photographing the many classic motels, cafés, and service stations along the route. I bought every book about Route 66 that I could get my hands on and read everything available on the history of the road. Around 1998, when I began collecting postcards of the route, it occurred to me that many of the places depicted on the postcards were either long gone or in danger of becoming lost to fast-food establishments, self-storage businesses, and mini malls. I began to get the idea of traveling to the sites pictured on the postcards and photographing them. As the project grew, I realized that it was important to record as many of these sites as possible before they were forever lost in the name of "progress." Future generations that might never have a chance to experience the Mother Road could look back and re-live a Route 66 road trip, if only in the pages of a book. The only problem was finding all of the vintage postcards I would need to make the project work.

I contacted collectors around the country and, to my surprise, all were willing to loan me their cards. In cases where postcards were not available of sites that I wanted to include in this book, I spoke with the owners of the properties and tried to acquire archival photos of these landmarks. I would like to thank the following people who allowed me access to their personal collections: Marion Clark, Earl and the late Cheryl Cory, Laurel Kane, Jeff Meyer, Steven Rider, Jim Ross, Mike Ward, and a very special thanks to Joe Sonderman. Without their help, this book could not have been made. I would also like to thank Brett Bather for all his encouragement during the making of this book.

After a year of gathering the cards and photos it was time to decide which sites I would use. It was a difficult task—all of them are important pieces of history that deserve to be cataloged. I had about 400 subjects to choose from, but had to narrow it down to 75 to fit the publisher's requirements. After the editing process, it was time to hit the road. The actual photography took place in June and July 2003. I began early one morning in Ludlow, California, but toward the end of the day experienced camera malfunctions and ended up spending a couple of days in a Kingman, Arizona, motel room while my camera was repaired back in Los Angeles. On the third day, after photographing the Meteorite Museum in Arizona, I experienced car problems and needed a tow to Holbrook. Unfortunately, it was a Saturday morning, and although it was only a minor radiator hose problem, all of Holbrook's garages were closed for the weekend. Again, I found a motel and sat around until Monday, when I found a mechanic. After a few hours I was again on my way. The rest of the trip went fairly smoothly, without any major problems.

The original idea was to take each shot from the exact spot that the postcard or archival photo was taken from. After the first day of shooting, however, I realized that that was not going to be possible. In many cases, the road had been widened, and standing in the middle of the road to shoot the photo was not an option. I also found that many of the buildings that I had planned to shoot had been expanded, or that trees had grown in, making the same angles virtually impossible. A few shots had to be altered simply because a freeway was built on top of the site where the photographer had taken the original postcard photograph. Every site I photographed presented its own unique problem. For perspective, look for small clues on the buildings like window patterns and backgrounds.

Also, as you read the book and go from state to state, imagine the many challenges that confronted early motorists who traveled Route 66. Imagine praying it does not rain while you're driving the treacherous Jericho Gap in Texas. Imagine worrying how far it is to the next service station because your gas gauge reads "E" and all that can be seen ahead is the black expanse of the nighttime desert. Traveling during the early days of motoring was an adventure. The places represented in this book were but a few of the many on Route 66 that fulfilled various needs for tourists and for travelers. I sincerely hope that some sense of that history and adventure comes through in the words and photographs presented in this book.

INTRODUCTION

U.S. HIGHWAY 66: AMERICA'S MAIN STREET

America has always been a nation of people on the go. While the methods of transportation have changed over the years, the goal remains.

Route 66 has its roots in the nation's old wagon trails. In 1857 Congress commissioned Lieutenant Edward Fitzgerald Beale to survey the land along the 35th Parallel from Fort Defiance near the New Mexico–Arizona border to the Colorado River. This route became known as Beale's Wagon Road, establishing a vital communication link to the West and serving as a military transport highway. Beale's Wagon Road, the Pontiac Trail in Illinois, the Ozark Trail in Missouri, and the old Santa Fe Trail were all in some form predecessors of what would become America's Main Street.

The turn of the twentieth century brought the burgeoning popularity of the automobile. Early automobile roads were primarily converted wagon trails and poorly marked, or not marked at all. As more and more people began using automobiles it became obvious that newer and better roads were needed. Grassroots "good road"

organizations and associations began popping up all over the country with the intent of improving roads and marking and mapping them.

By the mid-1920s about 250 marked trails existed across the country, all sponsored by local trail organizations. Since there wasn't a central organization coordinating these efforts, each association marked their trails in their own way. Some used painted stripes on fence posts, while others used symbols like the Indian head that guided folks along the Pontiac Trail in Illinois. These somewhat random and often overlapping markings created nightmares for early travelers. In 1924 the secretary of agriculture selected a board of state and federal highway officials to standardize a national highway numbering system and to explore the existing trails for possible use as part of a national highway system. Cyrus Avery, a state highway commissioner in Oklahoma, was among the officials selected to sit on the American Association of State Highway Officials. He worked with the chief engineer from Illinois, Frank Sheets, and chief engineer from Missouri, B. H. Piepmeier, on a proposed highway from Chicago to

Los Angeles. The proposed project was met with strong opposition because it was not considered a "tourist" route. (The fact that Avery routed the highway through his hometown didn't help matters.) Nevertheless, Avery and his associates believed strongly that this highway would become one of the country's most important highways. "There is more travel between Los Angeles and Chicago, or in that vicinity, than any other transcontinental route," Piepmeier wrote to Avery.

When it came time to number the road, the board chose 60 because all of the system's primary roads being planned were designated with numbers ending in zero. Officials in charge of the route from Virginia Beach to Springfield, Missouri, however, were also hoping to use that number and put up a fight to have their highway designated U.S. Highway 60. The disagreement continued for months until Avery and his associates eventually settled on the number 66 at the urging of Thomas H. MacDonald, chief of the Bureau of Public Roads, who was tired of the bickering. In November 1926, after two years of diligent work, the highway design and numbering system developed by Cyrus Avery and his associates was approved and set into motion.

Highway 66 followed a nontraditional diagonal path across Illinois, Missouri, Kansas, Oklahoma, Texas, New Mexico, Arizona, and California. The early route was made up of existing roads that zigzagged along county lines from town to town and state to state.

Individual states were for the most part responsible for road improvements and repairs from 1926 until 1933. In 1929 Highway 66 was fully paved in Illinois and Kansas. Missouri had 66 percent paved road and in Oklahoma 25 percent of the highway was hard road. In the western states early U.S. Highway 66 remained a primitive dirt byway with the exception of stretches in California's larger cities. Of 66's 1,200 miles west of Oklahoma, only 64.1 miles were paved.

By 1933 the federal government was taking an increased interest in the National Highway System, and President Franklin Roosevelt's New Deal program played a major role in the improvement of the nation's highways. From 1933 to 1938 the WPA (Works Progress Administration) and the CCC (Civilian Conservation Corps) worked to improve and maintain the National Highway System. By late 1937 the entire length of U.S. Highway 66 from Chicago to Los Angeles was paved.

With the country suffering economic depression, Midwestern farmers were hit with another disaster. A severe lack of rain coupled with strong winds turned farms in Oklahoma, Kansas, and Arkansas into a wasteland. An estimated 210,000 people left their homes behind during the so-called Dust Bowl and headed to California in search of a better life. Highway 66 became a road of flight and the path of choice for most of these farm families. John Steinbeck's 1939 novel *The Grapes of Wrath* immortalized the Dust Bowlers, forever linking them with Highway 66 and declaring the highway "The Mother Road."

During World War II Route 66 served as a main artery for military transportation and several installations were set up along or near Route 66. Between 1941 and 1943 more than 50 percent of all defense-related material needed for America's war production was transported and delivered by truck. At the onset of the war the government invested heavily in projects throughout California, primarily in the Los Angeles and San Diego areas. By 1943 a half million men and women were needed to meet production demands created by the war. With California's workforce depleted, people from outside the state filled most of these jobs. This new workforce traveled to California and new lives via Highway 66.

After World War II and the demise of gas and tire rationing, automobile travel exploded and the nation's busiest east-to-west highway overflowed. Hundreds of motels, cafés, and service stations sprang up along the entire route, ready to serve the increasingly mobile public. But the sudden influx of tourist travel and the lingering effects of heavy truck traffic during World War II took their toll on the road. By the early 1950s most of Highway 66 was too narrow to handle modern trucks and automobiles and was fast becoming obsolete. In 1956 the Federal Aid Highway Act was passed to provide expanded funding for the National Highway System, marking the end for America's Main Street. Newer four-lane roads built to Interstate standards began to open as early as 1958, and continued as rural areas were improved first, followed by town bypasses. As

construction neared each small village and town many business owners who ran roadside tourist services simply closed their doors in anticipation of the worst. Some stayed, however, and saw traffic through their respective towns slow to a trickle.

Business owners along the route usually remember the exact time of day the Interstate opened around their towns. Most compare the experience to the closing of a water faucet. One day hundreds of cars passed in front of their businesses; the next day a dozen or so might pass. Businesses struggled, but most eventually failed, and by the late 1970s most of the route had been replaced. On October 13, 1984, Williams, Arizona, became the last town along Route 66 to succumb, and in 1985 the fabled U.S. Highway 66 was officially decommissioned and all remaining signage removed.

For close to 50 years Route 66 was the caretaker of dreams for thousands of people. It took five Interstates to replace Route 66: Interstate 55 from Chicago to St. Louis, Interstate 44 from St. Louis to Oklahoma City, Interstate 40 from Oklahoma City to Barstow, Interstate 15 from Barstow to San Bernardino, and Interstate 10 from San Bernardino to Santa Monica. Maybe one day a hundred years from now people will look at the Interstates with this same feeling of nostalgia and wonder, as their tireless hovercraft speed over obsolete roads and diners serve their favorite food via plastic tubes. Until that day arrives, take a page from songwriter Bobby Troup, circa 1946: "If you ever plan to motor west/Travel my way, take the highway that's the best."

ILLINOIS

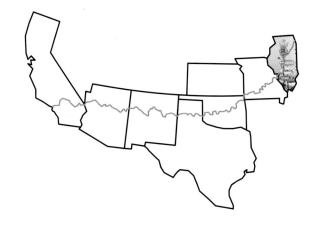

At the turn of the century roads and highways in the state of Illinois were primitive at best and impossible to navigate at worst. The history and development of Route 66 in Illinois can be traced back to these primitive roads and trails. In 1915 the main artery between Chicago and St. Louis was known as the Pontiac Trail, named for the eighteenth century chief of the Ottawa tribe. The trail was officially marked that same year with mile-by-mile guideposts from Chicago to St. Louis (courtesy of the B. F. Goodrich Company) ensuring even the novice traveler of at least having a chance of arriving at the proper destination. In 1918 a bond issue was passed for construction of hard roads in Illinois. The Pontiac Trail was designated SBI 4 (State Bond Issue) and began at 48th and Ogden in the western Chicago suburb of Cicero. After years of politicking and bureaucratic red tape, most of the road was finally paved by 1924, and by 1926 it was entirely a "hard road." The American Association of State Highway Officials approved the road for a U.S. Route designation and in 1927 U.S. Highway 66 signs were posted along its entire length.

Over the years many major changes took place to the routing of Route 66 in Illinois. In 1933 the easternmost terminus was moved from Cicero farther east to the entrance of Grant Park at Jackson Boulevard in Chicago. Another change took place in 1955 when Jackson became a one-way street and the official starting point was moved one block north to Adams Street, making the official endpoint the intersection of Jackson and Lake Shore Drive. In 1931 the original routing that followed Illinois Route 4 from Springfield to Staunton was rerouted to the east from Springfield to Litchfield, continuing to Mt. Olive. Another realignment occurred in the early 1930s when the route through Joliet and Wilmington was changed to alternate status and primary Highway 66 was redirected through Plainfield then on to Gardner, where the two versions of the route merged. As commercial truck traffic swelled and automobile traffic exploded throughout the late 1940s and into the 1950s, two-lane 66 was constantly improved and updated, and by 1957 the route was by and large a four-lane highway. The added improvements helped solve the congestion and safety problems but were no cure; it became painfully evident that Route 66 was outdated. It was the beginning of the end of the Mother Road in Illinois. By the mid-1970s most of Route 66 had been replaced with the new and modern Interstate 55. On January 17, 1977, the Illinois Department of Transportation removed the signs from the easternmost terminus, marking the official end of Route 66 in Illinois.

Today's traveler can still find much of the charm of old Route 66 in Illinois as they drive south from the towering concrete caverns of downtown Chicago, to the suburbs of Cicero and La Grange, and on through plains towns like Godley, Gardner, Dwight, Odell, Cayuga, Pontiac, Chenoa, Towanda, Funks Grove, Atlanta, Broadwell, Glenarm, Farmersville, Litchfield, Hamel, and Mitchell. To some, these small communities may be little more than dots on a map, but make no mistake: every town, motel, service station, mechanic, café, waitress, and short-order cook along the highway played an important role in shaping the history of Route 66 in Illinois.

WISHING WELL MOTEL, La GRANGE
c. 1946

The Wishing Well Motel was built by John Blackburn in 1941 at the corner of Route 66 (now Joliet Road) and Brainard Avenue, just 15 miles from the heart of downtown Chicago. When built, the motel consisted of 10 cabins, an office, and a small house out back. Blackburn later sold the property to the Bronsons, who in turn sold it to Emil and Zora Vidas in 1958. In 1960 the individual cabins were connected to increase capacity, and in 1983 the property underwent more remodeling with the addition of four units. The small house in back was also converted to guest quarters, upping the room count to 19. In 1985 Zoras's husband Emil passed away and Zora has been manager and caretaker ever since.

For 62 years the Wishing Well has treated its guests to a quiet, country-like atmosphere just out of shouting range of the big city. In the early 1960s the nearby Willowbrook Ballroom booked swing and dance bands for months at a time and the Wishing Well became a home away from home for the musicians. Members of the rock band Chicago were also guests in the early 1970s, although Zora was admittedly quite hesitant about renting to "those kids with that long hair." Through its many renovations and improvements, the Wishing Well has managed to keep its charm, and it still readily serves weary travelers each night. And, yes, there is an above-ground stone well on the premises.

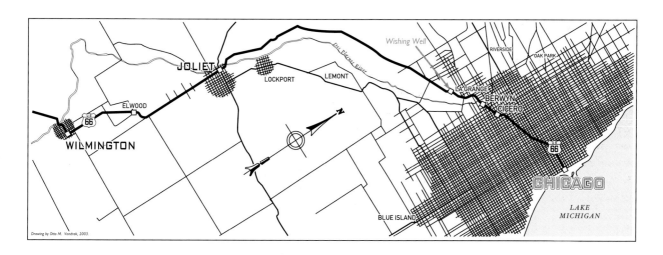

Drawing by Otto M. Vondrak, 2003.

THE RIVIERA, GARDNER
c. 1946

Established in 1928 by James Girot, a businessman from nearby South Wilmington, the Riviera Restaurant and Tavern is located on Route 66 (now Route 53) 60 miles south of Chicago. Buildings from the towns of Gardner (a church) and South Wilmington (a coal mine office) were moved and combined on-site to form the Riviera, which during its heyday also featured a zoo, picnic grounds, and a swimming hole, with the picturesque Mazon River just a couple of yards away. At the height of its popularity, the Rivera's restaurant was located upstairs, serving homemade Italian food, chicken, steak, and seafood. The lower portion of the building was a tavern.

The Riviera is rich in Route 66 history and Chicago gangster lore.

Al Capone and his brother Ralph often wet their whistles in the downstairs speakeasy after checking on their stills in nearby Kankakee County. Gene Kelly was also a frequent customer. In 1933 a gasoline station was added but was eventually shut down. In 1972 Bob and Peggy Kraft purchased the Riviera from the Girots and have carried on the Riviera tradition of good food and drink. The restaurant and tavern are now both downstairs. The food is transferred from the upstairs kitchen via a dumbwaiter. Walking into the now-combined restaurant and tavern, visitors are instantly transported to another time when flappers and jazz music were the rage and the speakeasy was the place to get a drink and socialize with friends.

LOG CABIN INN, PONTIAC
c. 1939

On the north side of the onetime coal-mining town of Pontiac, Illinois, sits the venerable Log Cabin Inn, a restaurant built by Joe and Victor Selotti in 1926 of cedar telephone poles. The Log Cabin, which seats 45 diners, has changed little since this part of the highway was the main thoroughfare between Chicago and St. Louis. The interior walls are made of knotty pine, projecting the feel of an old time café—the cars outside provide the only clues this is not 1939. The Log Cabin Inn was once best known for its beef, barbecued over open charcoal; Joe did the barbecuing in a separate building with windows that allowed customers to watch.

The path of Route 66 originally ran on the eastern side of the restaurant next to the railroad tracks. When the road was realigned to the western side, the building was raised and rotated with horses so the front door once again faced the road. It was quite an event that brought out half the town to watch. Other than turning the building around, the only major change to the restaurant over the years was the addition of a front entry in 1990. Gina Manker, a waitress who has worked at the Log Cabin Inn on and off for 30 years, says her favorite time to work is in the very early morning when the farmers come in for their coffee. When asked why, she blushes and says, "Oh my, the things you hear!"

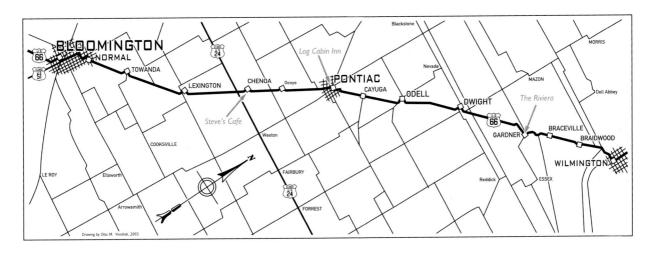

Drawing by Otto M. Vondrak, 2003.

STEVE'S CAFÉ, CHENOA
c. 1950

The building that eventually housed Steve's Café was built in 1918 and was originally called Wahls Brothers. Steve's Café came about in the 1930s when new owner Steve Wilcox took over. People in the area still speak in reverence when referring to the pie and coffee served at Steve's. A Texaco service station was later added to the business. A canopy was added and the station was fully enclosed in the early 1970s. The Texaco station closed shortly thereafter and around 1975 that section of the building was turned into a bar called the Red Bird Lounge, named for the local Chenoa Red Birds high school sports teams. In 1975 Ken and Peg Sipe took over the building and continued to serve home-cooked meals and "World Famous Pie." During the summers, Steve's Café sponsored Friday-night fish fries at the local park. Peggy desperately tried to keep the café open after her husband was killed in an auto accident but eventually had to close the doors in 1997 after 22 years in business. Since the café's closure it has seen service as a used-car lot and an antique shop. Les Stevens, a Chenoa police officer, says what he remembers most about Steve's was the "huge steak-and-eggs breakfast with potatoes and the works for $3.99." The old cafe currently sits quietly on old 66, clinging to its past and hoping for a future.

STEVE'S CAFE INTERSECTION CITY 66 & 24 CHENOA, ILLINOIS

DIXIE TRUCKERS HOME, McLEAN
c. LATE 1940s

J. P. Walters and his son-in-law, John Geske, built the Dixie Truckers Home in 1928 at the intersection of U.S. Routes 66 and 138 in McLean, Illinois. Housed in a rented garage, the first incarnation of the café had only a counter and six stools. Throughout its history, the Dixie Truckers Home has been constantly improved and remodeled. In the late 1930s six tourist cabins were added and eventually the café was expanded to serve 60 people. In 1965 a grease fire in the kitchen, aided by wooden exhaust ducts, destroyed the café. Amazingly, the tourist cabins and gas pumps were unscathed. In fact, that very evening, the gas pumps were back in business and one of the cabins was pressed into service as a temporary home for the café. The new Dixie Truckers Home reopened two years later with the capacity to serve 250 hungry travelers. The Dixie Truckers Home was not only consistently ranked among the nation's top 10 truck stops, serving customers with that southern hospitality its name implied, it was also home to the Route 66 Hall of Fame and Museum. At the time of this writing, the longtime family-owned truck stop was sold to a company based in Providence, Rhode Island, which planned to change the Dixie's name to Dixie Travel Plaza.

REDWOOD MOTEL, LINCOLN
c. 1965

Construction of the Redwood Motel began in 1955 and its first guests were welcomed in 1956. Built by Wilfred and Dorothy Werth, the Redwood sat conveniently at the junction of Routes 66, 10, and 21, with 15 rooms and a small living quarters attached to the main building. The exterior of the motel was originally constructed of stone and redwood, but by 1960 so many stones were falling off the walls that Wilfred decided to brick the entire exterior. The cost to stay at the Redwood in 1956 was $5 for a single and $8 for a double. When television was installed the rates were raised to $6 and $10, respectively.

In 1934, 22 years prior to opening the motel, Wilfred had built a Standard Oil station on the same corner. Wilfred proudly states that he had the "first gasoline pumps in the state that showed the dollars and cents through the small windows on the pumps." Wilfred, who turned 87 in 2003, adds that he and Dorothy "had fun" owning the motel but sold it in 1963 when Ruth Buckles made an offer he couldn't refuse. The station was sold in 1991 and is today a Quick Lube. The original motel sign was torn down after high winds ripped off a few letters, says current lessee Sherman West, and was replaced with a new sign in November 2002. Sherman and wife Joan have plans to renovate the entire motel, hoping to make it a "must" stop for travelers on Old 66.

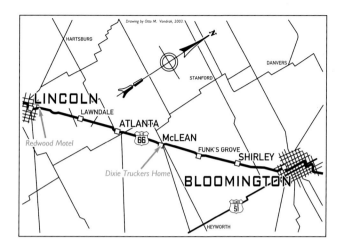

ERNIE'S PIG HIP, BROADWELL
c. 1972

Ernie Edwards opened what would become the famous Pig Hip Restaurant in 1937 with three tables, a bar, $150 of borrowed money, and a desire to be his own boss. At first the restaurant was called the Harbor Inn because of a great deal Ernie found on wallpaper and restaurant glasses with a nautical theme. The name was shortlived. One day a hungry farmer came into the restaurant and spied a freshly baked ham on the stove. He pointed to the ham and said, "Give me a slice o' that pig hip." The rest, as they say, is history. Ernie applied for a patent on his sandwich (a generous helping of thinly sliced ham smothered with Pig Hip sauce) and copyrighted the name Pig Hip.

The sandwich was so popular that he opened two more restaurants in nearby towns but eventually closed them when he realized that managing two more Pig Hips was more than he had bargained for.

Ernie finally hung up his chef's hat and carving knife in 1991 after 54 years of serving up a local legend. With the help of the Illinois Route 66 Preservation Committee, Ernie's Pig Hip restaurant was transformed into a Route 66/Pig Hip Museum in late spring 2003, with 700 attending opening day. The Pig Hip's slogan, "The sandwich with the secret sauce: It made its way by the way it's made," was a fitting tribute to Ernie Edwards and his famous sandwich.

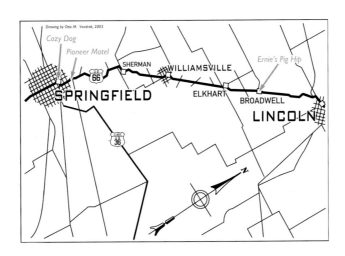

PIONEER MOTEL, SPRINGFIELD
c. 1940s

The classic Pioneer Motel sits on the north end of Springfield, beckoning to cars passing by on historic 66. This small motel was built in the 1940s close to Route 66 and the Route 66 city bypass and was highly rated by AAA. The Pioneer initially consisted of 12 units arranged in the classic L-shape style, with parking in front of each room. Sometime after the original construction, an archway was built over the driveway at the front office for guest safety, and a living room was added to the office space. At one time a small motel existed adjacent to the Pioneer but was eventually purchased by the owners of the Pioneer. The added rooms increased the Pioneer's total guest rooms to 21. The motel currently rents many units out by the month but keeps a few open for overnight guests looking to spend the night at a vintage Route 66 motel. One of the current owners, Teresa Roberts, says plans are in the works to renovate the motel. This, she says, will "hopefully attract more interest to the Pioneer Motel from travelers and fans of Route 66." Although the motel has gone through several ownership changes over the years, the name was never changed and to this day the classic MOTEL sign tower above the office continues to greet guests.

COZY DOG DRIVE IN, SPRINGFIELD
c. 1950

Ed Waldmire Jr. and his friend Don Strand developed the Cozy Dog while stationed in Amarillo, Texas, during World War II. To earn extra money, Ed sold the new-fangled food—a delectable combination of a hot dog on a stick dipped in special batter and French-fried—at the USO club and at the base PX. The "Crusty Curs," as they were first known, quickly became a local favorite. After Ed's discharge from the military he introduced the "dogs" to the public at the 1946 Illinois State Fair; they were such a hit that Ed decided to sell his new fast food in his hometown of Springfield, Illinois.

The first Cozy Dog stand was opened at the Lake Springfield beach house on June 16 of that same year. At the insistence of his wife Virginia, who wondered who would eat something called a "Crusty Cur," Ed began kicking around ideas for a new name. After much painstaking thought, "Cozy Dog" was settled upon. A second Cozy Dog stand was opened on Ash and MacArthur in Springfield, and in 1950 Waldmire moved into a building that shared seating with the local Dairy Queen. In 1976, Ed's son Buz and daughter-in-law Sue leased the restaurant from Ed. After their divorce, Buz sold his half to Sue, who has run the restaurant ever since. The Cozy Dog moved to its current location at 2935 South 6th Street in 1996 and sits partially on the property of the former Route 66 landmark Lincoln Motel.

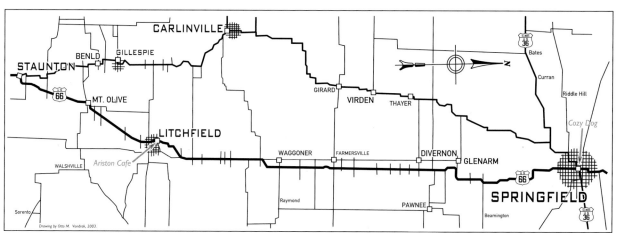

ARISTON CAFÉ, LITCHFIELD
c. 1935

Ariston Café, opened by Pete Adam in the town of Carlinville in 1924, consisted of a small café with a few gas pumps out front. In 1926, Route 66 was given official designation and routed through the small Illinois town, and Adam's business flourished. In 1931, however, Highway 66 was re-routed east through Litchfield and business suffered. Not one to give up, Pete moved the Ariston to Litchfield. Business boomed again and in 1935 he found it necessary to construct a larger building. This "new" café, which holds more than 100 hungry customers, stands today pretty much as it did when it was built almost 70 years ago. Over the years, 66 was rerouted several times through Litchfield. Each change made it necessary to move the front door of the restaurant to keep it facing the road. As fate would have it, with the last realignment the restaurant entrance wound up at the original front location.

The Ariston is a well-known stop along Route 66 and has been a family-run operation since opening its doors. Nick and Demi Adam are proud of the café's history and its connection with the Mother Road, and continue the fine tradition that began 80 years ago. "We continue to believe in offering the highest quality selection of food, while providing the first-rate service that you expect," they say, "and at a price that continues to bring our valued customers back time and time again."

MISSOURI

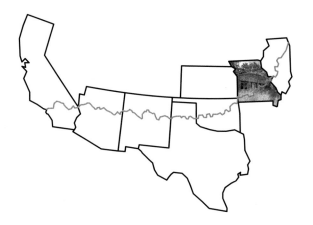

Route 66 leaves the Illinois plains and crosses into Missouri at the Mississippi River. It then cuts diagonally across Missouri from St. Louis to the high plains southwest of Springfield. As it slices through the Ozarks, the highway follows approximately the same route as a stage line established by the U.S. government two decades before the Civil War. During the Civil War, this trail was an important military thoroughfare traveled by Union and Confederate troops alike. It was during that time the federal government installed a telegraph line along the road with stations at St. Louis, Rolla, Lebanon, Marshfield, and Springfield. The old stage line, previously known as the Kickapoo Trail, the Osage Trace, the Springfield Road, and the Military Road, thus became known as the Old Wire Road or Telegraph Road.

At Springfield, the road connected with what would become the Ozark Trail, headed west, and eventually terminated in Santa Rosa, New Mexico. The Ozark Trails Association established the Ozark Trail in 1915, and in August 1922, the newly formed Missouri State Highway Commission designated seven roads totaling about 1,500 miles as primary roads throughout the state, including State Route 14, the future U.S. Highway 66, laid on the former Old Wire Road. Work on the new highway progressed at a rapid pace, and on January 5, 1931, the last section of hard top was completed in Pulaski County, making Missouri the third of the eight Route 66 states to complete its paving through the entire state.

The new road helped Missouri flourish and become one of the most popular vacation destinations in the country. Rivers, lakes, and a wealth of forestland attracted sportsmen from around the nation. Travelers and vacationers alike found an abundance of motels, resorts, and lodges to choose from. These vacation destinations came in all sizes and shapes, but none were more recognizable than the stylized stone or "rocked" buildings that proliferated in the Ozarks.

Highly skilled "rock men," as they were called, carefully cut and placed slabs of colorful sandstone over the frames of buildings, creating the unique look often called "giraffe stone." At the height of its popularity in the late 1930s and into the late 1940s, scores of motels, cafés, gas stations, and homes were rocked in this style. Many examples of this style still exist along Route 66 in the Ozarks region, including the Wagon Wheel Motel featured in this chapter.

Also popular in Missouri were the abundant caves and caverns that became tourist attractions over the years. Signs painted on barns to advertise the caverns became common sights throughout the Midwest on Route 66. By the time travelers arrived in Missouri, they were almost literally brainwashed into stopping. As an incentive, one cave owner, Lester Dills of Meremec Caverns in Stanton, offered to paint farmers' barns for free if they allowed him to advertise on them. Not many refused his offer.

As in the other states through which Route 66 passes, the road underwent many alignment changes in Missouri. Roads were straightened to make them safer, towns were bypassed to create faster routes, and two-lane Route 66 was eventually upgraded to four lanes. With the passage of the Federal Highway Aid Act in 1956, Missouri began work almost immediately on its new Interstate. Lebanon holds the dubious honor of being the first town in Missouri to be bypassed by the new highway. By the dawn of the 1980s Interstate 44 had replaced most of Route 66 across the Show-Me State; a section of the highway at Devils Elbow was the last to be bypassed in 1981. Even so, many surviving stretches of old Route 66 still exist today and can be driven and explored. Many of the small towns and villages there still retain that old-time feel and vintage charm of the Mother Road's glory days. They're all just an Interstate exit away.

THE DIAMONDS, VILLA RIDGE
c. 1948

Location, location, location—the key to success for any restaurant. At the junction of Routes 50, 66, and 100, The Diamonds utilized all three. Spencer Groff knew he had an envious location when he opened the first Diamonds on July 3, 1927. As word spread the restaurant quickly became known from coast to coast for fine food and courteous service. In 1948 a spectacular fire destroyed the original Diamonds and traffic was brought to a halt in both directions on Route 66 for hours as smoke covered the road. Groff and business partner Louis Eckelkamp (who also owned the nearby Gardenway Motel) rebuilt the Diamonds in an ultramodern streamlined style alongside 25 cottages and a swimming pool. In 1967 Interstate 44 bypassed the area and The Diamonds and its facilities were moved to new buildings farther east near the I-44 access ramp at Gray Summit. Interstate construction also forced the closure of the Tri-County Truck Stop 20 miles west in Sullivan. Owners Arla and Roscoe Reed in 1971 chose the abandoned Diamonds building to house the new Tri-County Truck Stop. Ironically, the relocated Diamonds Restaurant, once billed as the "World's Largest Roadside Restaurant," is now closed and abandoned, while the Tri-County Truck Stop remains open on the site of the second Diamonds, and continues to serve hungry truckers and tourists traveling I-44 and Route 66.

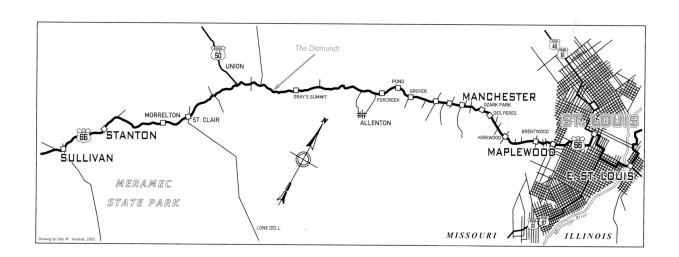

WAGON WHEEL MOTEL, CUBA
c. 1934

The Wagon Wheel Motel on the eastern end of Cuba is one of the most recognizable landmarks on Route 66. Originally known as the Wagon Wheel Cabin Court, it was built by Robert and Margaret Martin, with local stonemason Leo Friescenhan hired as designer and construction supervisor. Originally a nine-room motel, Ozark Stone and brick trim on the windows and porches give it the classic "rocked" look that was popular in the region. The Wagon Wheel once boasted "All modern steam heated, fireproof cottages," as was printed on the back of this postcard. In the 1930s rooms rented for $1.50 and up per night. By 1946 the motel had expanded to 14 units, a number that grew to 18 when the garages were enclosed and converted. A service station and 24-hour café were also on the property, but were owned independently of the motel.

When I-44 bypassed the area in the late 1960s the motel's future looked bleak, but the Wagon Wheel managed to hang on. The motel has had several owners during its lifetime (one of them, a Mr. Mathis, designed the very recognizable neon sign), but Harold and Pauline Armstrong, owners for more than 40 years, attribute continued success to clean, quiet rooms at a great price. Venerable longtime caretaker Roy Mudd, who has been tending to the property for forty years, is as much a part of the classic motel as the neon sign and the Ozark stone.

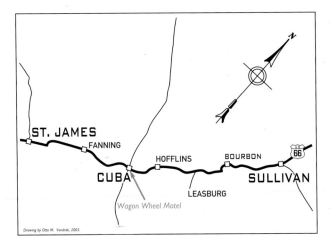

Drawing by Otto M. Vondrak, 2003.

ROLLA
c. 1940s

Rolla originated in 1855 when a group of contractors engaged in construction of the St. Louis, San Francisco Railway (aka "the Frisco") selected the area for supply warehouses and a railway office. According to legend, a local resident named George Coopedge, who was homesick for his native North Carolina, suggested the name Raleigh. The name was accepted and the decision was made to spell it exactly the way George pronounced it. The concrete paving of two-lane Route 66 through Missouri was completed in 1931 and was greeted by the citizens of Rolla with a huge public celebration that included a grand parade. There was cause for a celebration as the new and improved roadway meant increased traffic through town, which resulted in a much-needed boost for business at the local cafés, service stations, and motels that lined the town's main street. A couple of miles west of town in 1925, on the site of an old pioneer cabin, was built the Old Homestead, which today stands as one of the country's first truck stops.

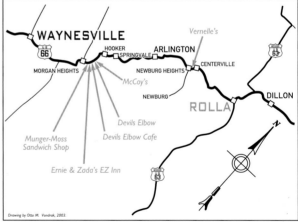

VERNELLE'S MOTEL, NEWBURG
c. 1952

In 1938 E. P. Gasser built a store, filling station, novelty shop, and six cabins on this property and named it Gasser Tourist Court. Fred and Vernelle Gasser bought the property from Fred's uncle in 1952 and added a restaurant and motel there. The restaurant seated 100 people and was well known for chicken-fried steak and open-faced roast beef sandwiches. The expansion of Route 66 to four lanes in 1957 necessitated the relocation of the restaurant and several other buildings. The motel was bought by Nye Goodridge in the early 1960s and is still owned and operated by his son Ed, who once worked in the restaurant as a cook and did "a little bit of everything" while his wife Jean worked as a waitress. According to Ed, the restaurant was torn down around 1968 when Interstate 44 came through. Three units were added to the motel, however, bringing the total to 17.

Once again, Vernelle's, which has endured its share of setbacks, is on shaky ground. The state of Missouri deemed unsafe I-44 in this area, and announced that it will relocate it behind the motel, a project scheduled to take several years. Sadly, this will leave Vernelle's and its sign with no visibility from the Interstate and most likely will mark the end of another classic family-operated Route 66 motel. "We're going to be off the road," says Ed. "No visibility here at all. They are cutting our throats." Progress is a matter of opinion. Just ask Ed.

DEVILS ELBOW
c. 1939

Devils Elbow is a quiet, picturesque village on the Big Piney River about 20 miles west of Rolla. Listed as one of Missouri's top scenic spots, this Ozarks town was named by lumberjacks who floated logs down to this treacherous portion of the river. The logs would often jam at the bend and cause long delays, leading the rafters to comment that the river at this point had a "devil of an elbow."

A block east of the bridge leading into Devils Elbow sits the Elbow Inn (originally Munger-Moss Sandwich Shop). Across the bridge is the site of the old Devils Elbow Café and the Conoco station built by Dwight Rench in 1932. The café and station were at one time affiliated with the nearby Cedar Lodge, 10 cabins boasting private cooking facilities. The café housed the local post office from 1931 to 1941, and in later years was transformed into a tavern called The Hideaway, which burned to the ground in the late 1950s. A block from the café was McCoy's Store and Camp, an old-fashioned general store built by Charles McCoy in 1941. In addition to selling fishing tackle and sporting goods, McCoy's rented boats for use on the Big Piney, as well as six small sleeping rooms upstairs; the

Devils Elbow Cafe
Devils Elbow, Mo.

owners lived in a four-bedroom apartment downstairs behind the store. In 1948 seven small cabins were added, but McCoy's closed in 1954 and was turned into an apartment building.

That year, McCoy's son-in-law, Atholl "Jiggs" Miller, and his wife Dorothy built Millers Market, and sold camping essentials, dry goods, and gasoline. Jiggs was the postmaster until 1982 when he sold the market to Terry and Marilyn Allman, who operated the store as Allman's Market until October 2001, when the property was sold to Phil Sheldon, who changed the name to Sheldon's Market. Sheldon had managed The Hideaway for a year before entering the army in

1942. About a mile west of downtown sat Ernie and Zada's Inn, also known as the E-Z Inn. Built in the late 1930s it consisted of a Sinclair station, restaurant, and cabins and had a wild reputation as a honky-tonk. It closed after only a few years of operation, according to Sheldon. The building that once served as the gas station and restaurant is now a private residence.

In 1943 Route 66 bypassed the town was to accommodate heavy military traffic from nearby Fort Leonard Wood, and in the early 1980s Interstate 44 completely left Devils Elbow behind.

{ DANCING, FISHING, HUNTING, SHADY TRAILER CAMP, DINNERS, LUNCHES, BEER MODERN CABINS WITH IN-SPR. MATTRESS }

E161 ERNIE & ZADA'S INN HI-WAY 66 1 MILE WEST OF DEVIL'S ELBOW, MO. Schuster Studio Hermann, Mo.

McCOY'S
AT DEVIL'S ELBOW, MO.

MUNGER-MOSS
SANDWICH SHOP, DEVILS ELBOW
c. 1936

Nelle Munger and Emmett Moss built the Munger-Moss Sandwich Shop in 1936 soon after they married. The café was built on a piece of land that sits next to the picturesque bridge at the Big Piney River. Route 66 bypassed this location in 1943 when a new four-lane section was completed to accommodate heavy military traffic from nearby Fort Leonard Wood. As a result of the realignment, tourist traffic through the area was drastically reduced and business slowed to a crawl. The Munger-Moss Sandwich Shop then moved, along with its original owners, to a new location west of Devils Elbow in the town of Lebanon. In 1946, Paul and Nadine Thompson bought and reopened the old location and changed the name of the café to the Elbow Inn, which they successfully operated well into the 1960s. After its closure the café sat empty and at one time served as a private residence. It was reopened in 1997, again as the Elbow Inn, and has since gained quite a reputation for its outstanding barbecue.

S663   BIG PINEY RIVER,   HI-WAY 66,   DEVIL'S ELBOW   Schuster Studio

WAYNESVILLE
c. 1940s

Waynesville was established in 1833 as a simple trading post for settlers and trappers on the Roubidoux River, and was named for General "Mad" Anthony Wayne, a hero of the Revolutionary War. The stretch of Route 66 in this area can be traced back to the early 1800s when an overland trail was established between St. Louis and Springfield. The trail's various names spell out its history: Kickapoo Trail, the Osage Trace, Old Wire Road, Old Springfield Road, Highway 14, and eventually U.S Highway 66.

Many buildings in Waynesville survive from the 1920s and 1930s, including the former Bell Hotel (now Waynesville Memorial Chapel) built by Robert Bell. In anticipation of the coming tourist trade from the new Highway 66, Bell expanded his home in 1925 and turned it into the Bell Hotel. It operated until 1937 under the slogan "Every Facility for the Traveler's Pleasure – Old Southern Hospitality." Through the hard times of the 1920s and 1930s Waynesville's status as the seat of Pulaski County, combined with the ever-increasing tourist travel on Route 66, kept the town alive. In 1941 the construction of nearby Fort Leonard Wood brought thousands of military and construction workers to the area, and as World War II unfolded Waynesville became the primary place of recreation for men and women stationed on the base. Since then, Waynesville has had its share of ups and downs, good times and bad, but the friendliness and small-town ways have remained constant.

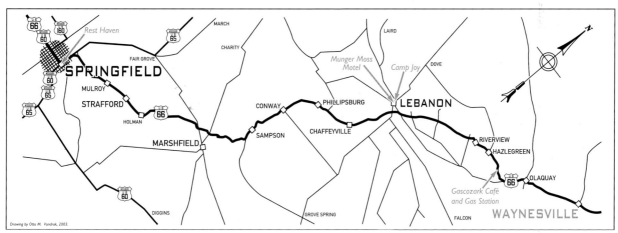

Drawing by Otto M. Vondrak, 2003.

GASCOZARK CAFÉ
AND GAS STATION, GASCOZARK
c. 1939

In 1931, Frank A. Jones built the Gascozark Café and Gas Station, which he owned and operated along with a popular tourist and fishing resort on the nearby Gasconade River. Jones, who originally settled in the area in the 1920s, in fact coined the town name "Gascozark" as a combination of *Gasconade* and Ozark. The former refers to the Gascony region of France that lent its name to the nearby river; the latter is a distortion of the French *Aux Arc. Aux* (sounds like "oh") means "to" and *arc* is short for one of the region's native tribes. "Ozark," hence, literally means "to the Arkansas."

As tourist traffic on Route 66 steadily increased, so did business at the café and Jones soon made additions to the main building. In the mid-1930s Rudy and Clara Schuermann bought and took over the business. In 1939 the Schuermanns hired a Mr. Lillard, a "rock man," who added the large Ozark stones around the front and sides to alleviate the patchy look of the main building and its add-ons. In the 1940s the Gascozark Café and Gas Station became a regular stop on the Greyhound bus line, providing a substantial boost in business. In the 1950s another transformation to the café took place when it became a local hot spot known as the Spinning Wheel Tavern. In later years the building served as a private residence but as of this writing it sits vacant.

CAMP JOY, LEBANON
c. 1930

Leaving Nebraska City, Nebraska, behind, Ernis and Lois Spears, accompanied by Ernis' parents, traveled back and forth on the new U. S. Highway 66 during the late 1920s in search of the perfect spot for a new tourist camp. Upon arriving in each town the two couples surveyed the area for possibilities, often spending days in one spot, counting passing cars. They found what they were looking for in Lebanon. Camp Joy, which began with 50-cents-a-night tent rentals, was so successful that Ernis and his father Charles built cabins. Eventually, attached carports were converted to drive-in garages and then to more rooms. As tourist travel increased so did tourist demands, and indoor plumbing in each cabin replaced a communal bathhouse.

By the end of 1935 Camp Joy featured 24 cabins that rented for $1.25 to $4, depending on the number of rooms. A gas station and café were added but were eventually moved to accommodate even more cabins. A drive-through archway read, "Camp Joy" on the entrance side and "Teach your baby to say Camp Joy" on the exit side. According to Joy Spears Fishel, Ernis and Lois's daughter, customers in the early days seemed more like friends than customers: "In the evenings after supper, people would get out and visit. TV made a big difference. TV and air conditioning. After those came in people didn't want to get together anymore." The Spears owned and operated the property until 1971. The few cabins still standing are now rented on a monthly basis

MUNGER MOSS MOTEL, LEBANON
c. 1950s

Jesse and Pete Hudson, onetime owners of the Munger Moss Sandwich Shop in Devils Elbow, relocated in Lebanon after Devils Elbow was bypassed. Property in Lebanon was purchased in 1945 and the Munger Moss Motor Court was built in 1946 and originally consisted of seven buildings housing two units each and a garage. Rooms rented for $3 a night. Eleven more buildings were eventually added along the semicircular driveway, adding 44 new rooms. As tourist business increased during the postwar era so did demand for more rooms. As with many motels of the era, the attached garages were converted into rooms. Television came to the area in the early 1950s and tacked an extra 50 cents to the room rate. A swimming pool, new office, and sign were added in the late 1950s; all three are still in use today.

Bob and Ramona Lehman bought the motel in 1971 and have been its caretakers ever since. Ramona has gloriously decorated a few of the rooms with Route 66 themes: Room 18 is the famous Coral Court Room, a must see for Route 66 enthusiasts. Room 66 is, of course, the Munger Moss Historic Room, filled with old photos and memorabilia. Illinois, Kansas, Oklahoma, and Missouri all have rooms decorated in their honor, and the motel is one of the cleanest and well kept along all of Route 66.

REST HAVEN
MOTOR COURT
SPRINGFIELD, MO.

MAY PHOTO

REST HAVEN MOTOR COURT, SPRINGFIELD
c. 1947

The Rest Haven Motor Court was built in 1947 by Hillary and Mary Brightwell and originally consisted of four rock cottages containing two rooms each, and a Phillips 66 service station out front. In 1953 a new two-story sign was added and is said to use 900 individual light bulbs. Many of the motels on Route 66 expanded at a furious pace during the postwar period and the Rest Haven was no exception. Ten more rock cottages were added in 1952, and in 1955 an additional 10 were built to meet the ever-growing demand. By that time the Rest Haven offered "100% Refrigerated Air Conditioning," telephones, free radios, ice, a well-equipped playground, and was recommended by Duncan Hines. The service station out front was dismantled in 1955 and reassembled at the rear of the property; today it is used for storage. In the early 1960s the gaps between the original four cottages were filled in to add three more rooms. A swimming pool was also installed in the 1960s. Hillary and Mary owned the motel and lived on site until 1979 when, after 32 years of greeting guests, they retired. In 1980 the Rest Haven was purchased by Mr. and Mrs. Pendya, who have been caretakers ever since. The Rest Haven remains a fine example of the well-kept, mom-and-pop motels that have survived despite the road's demise.

LOG CITY CAMP, AVILLA
c. 1940s

In 1926 Carl Stansbury built several log cabins 14 1/2 miles east of Carthage, Missouri, to start a business utilizing trees he cut down while clearing the land. Out front of Log City Camp he built a café made of stone, a gas station, and a store. By 1935 Stansbury had built "fourteen modern cottages with conveniences" that rented for $1 to $3 a night. The camp eventually expanded to include 16 cottages and cabins. On the back of this postcard Log City Camp advertised a "Dining room with coffee shop, air conditioned by washed air, serving excellent food at popular prices. You Name It, We've Got It." Log City also boasted Beautyrest mattresses in each cabin.

Two years after building Log City, rivals built the Forest Park Camp across the highway. Forest Park at the time comprised 10 rock cabins. Not to be outdone, Stansbury added three rock cabins of his own. When the owners of Forest Park built a café, Stansbury added a coffee shop to the Log City Camp. Stansbury also added a dining room, prompting his rivals across the highway to establish a tavern and dance hall. This "friendly" competition went on for years, with the owners of each camp trying to outdo the other. Eventually the new Interstate bypassed both camps. Just a single rock cabin remains across the highway at the former Forest Park Camp.

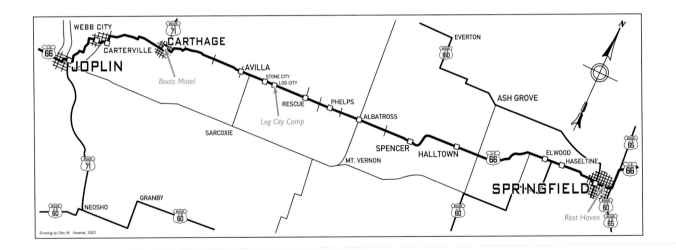

Drawing by Otto M. Vondrak, 2003.

LOG CITY CAMP
14½ MILES EAST OF CARTHAGE, M
ON HIGHWAY 66

DINING ROOM
LOG CITY CAMP
BLAKE
Photo

COTTAGE AT LOG CITY CAMP
ON HIGHWAY 66
14½ MILES EAST OF
CARTHAGE MO

BOOTS COURT, CARTHAGE
c. 1949

Situated at the corner of Route 66 and Highway 71 at the so-called "Crossroads of America" sits the Boots Motel, one of the most recognizable landmarks on all of Route 66. Built by Arthur Boots in 1939, the distinctly streamline moderne motel began with four units of two rooms each. Classic pink and green neon follow the graceful lines of the motel, and a covered driveway allows guests to park next to their rooms. A Mobil station that once sat out front was eliminated to make space for more rooms. Early advertising boasted of "A radio in every room," and Clark Gable is rumored to have stayed in Room 6 and signed the guest book, "Clark Gable and Party."

In 1942 Ples Nelly bought the Boots Motel and added five rooms at the rear of the complex. In 1948, Ruben and Rachel Asplin bought the property, longing to leave the cold winters of Minnesota behind. After Ruben's death, Rachel continued to run the motel until her death in 1991 at the age of 91. Current owner John Ferguson rents rooms on a weekly basis only, but still turns on the classic neon every night. The motel's listing on the National Register of Historic Places would be a shoo-in if not for the nonoriginal pitched roof that was added in later years. At the time of this writing Ferguson was hoping for a buyer to restore the Boots to its former glory.

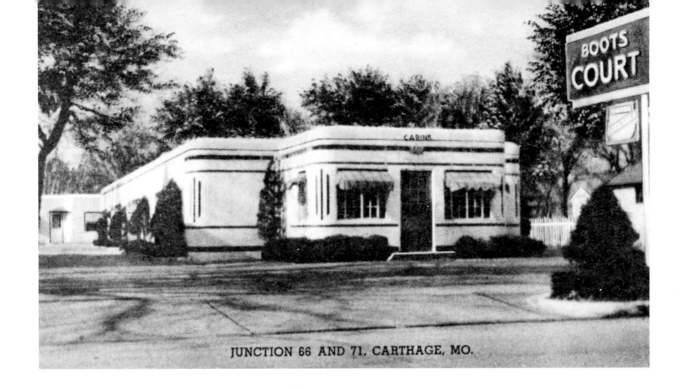

JUNCTION 66 AND 71, CARTHAGE, MO.

KANSAS

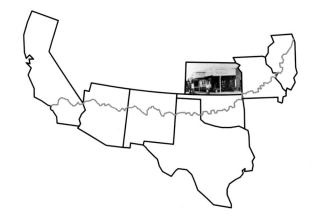

Of the 2,400 miles of Route 66 from Chicago to Los Angeles, Kansas accounts for a mere 13.2 miles. While cattle and the railroad played major roles in the economics of the region, this area of the state was ore-mining country from 1876 to around 1960. One lucky miner is said to have uncovered his fortune while sliding into first base during a baseball game. He quickly covered it up, leased the land that night, and began digging the next morning.

The first town one encounters along Route 66 in Kansas is Galena. Just before entering Galena is an area that looks a bit like a war-torn battle zone. Known as "Hell's Half Acre," piles of mining debris known as "chat" fill the landscape, a sobering reminder of past mining operations and the devastation it caused to the local environment. Many bloody union battles were also staged and fought in the region.

Just a few miles down 66 is Riverton, the onetime home of the world-famous Spring River Inn. Built in 1905, the Spring River began operation as a restaurant in 1952 and was destroyed by fire in the late 1990s. Still farther down the highway is Baxter Springs, "The First Cow Town in Kansas" and the site of the Baxter Springs Massacre. In October 1863 Lieutenant William Quantrill's Confederate troops, dressed in Union Army uniforms, ambushed an unknowing Union detachment and wagon train approaching the fort. One hundred three Union soldiers were killed, along with three Confederate soldiers. All are buried in a mass grave near the former site of the fort.

This part of Kansas boasts an abundance of rich and colorful history in which U.S Highway 66 played a major part. Tales of outlaw legends abound in these parts, including a well-known Jesse James bank robbery in the 1870s and frequent appearances by Bonnie Parker and Clyde Barrow more than 60 years later.

As the mining industry slowly dwindled the economy was bolstered by the influx of westbound travelers on Route 66. All three Kansas towns located along the Mother Road served travelers well. Those 13.2 miles in Kansas provide a virtual microcosm of the entire eight-state route; Galena, Riverton, and Baxter Springs were prime examples of the hundreds of small towns that dotted the length of the highway. During the Mother Road's heyday, their main streets were full of tourists filling their automobiles with gas or catching a quick bite at local cafés. Today, the streets are lined with classic architecture. Many a weary traveler too tired to drive another couple of miles to Oklahoma spent the night at Jayhawk Court in Riverton or the Capistrano Motel or Baxter Modern Cabins in Baxter Springs.

The lucrative tourist trade came to a sudden end when Interstate construction was completed in the area in the early 1960s, connecting I-44 in Missouri to the Will Rogers Turnpike in Oklahoma and leaving Kansas high and dry. In fact, Kansas holds the dubious distinction of being the only Route 66 state to be completely bypassed by the Interstate. It is also the only state not represented in Bobby Troup's hit song "Get Your Kicks on Route 66." The old route through Kansas remained a state road, however, and is today designated Kansas 66. Local residents are proud of their 13.2 miles and work hard to keep and preserve what is left.

GALENA
c. 1950s

Route 66 enters Galena over a gracefully curved overpass down to Front Street. After about half a mile, it takes a sharp left-hand turn onto Main Street. At one time Galena, named for a type of lead ore that often contained silver, had a reputation as a rowdy, untamed mining town complete with gamblers, swindlers, and drunkards. Main Street during the early 1900s mining boom was known as "Red Hot Street" and was full of saloons, gambling joints, and bawdy houses, all open 24 hours. Traveling down the sleepy Main Street today one would be hard-pressed to see any evidence of Galena's wild past. In 1935 striking United Mine Workers blocked Route 66 in front of the Eagle Picher Smelter and shot at drivers who ignored their commands. Sheriffs rerouted traffic and the governor declared martial law and sent in the National Guard. Labor unrest continued and reached a climax in 1937 when nine men were shot while demonstrating against union organization efforts. During the 1940s and 1950s local roadside businesses enjoyed steady streams of traffic and customers as America's Main Street also happened to be Galena's Main Street. Today, Main Street is home to a few local businesses but the damage caused by a dwindling mining industry and a Route 66 bypass is evident in the abandoned brick buildings that line the street. During the mining boom Galena's population ran as high as 25,000; today it hovers at around 4,000.

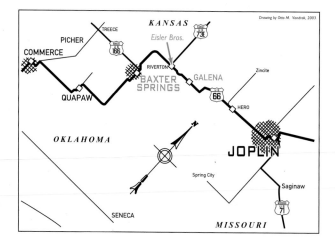

EISLER BROTHERS MARKET, RIVERTON
c. 1930s

On March 20, 1925 Leo Williams and his wife Lora opened a small roadside store on what was to become U.S. Highway 66 through Riverton. Fashioned after the "general" stores of the era, the Williams' store carried everything from clothes and shoes to milk, eggs, and fresh meat, as well as chili and barbecued beef that were cooked in a pit out back. A regulation croquet court was built on a lot adjacent to the store complete with lights for night play. Local tournaments became popular among area residents. As traffic continued to grow, business flourished and the court was dismantled to accommodate a parking lot.

In 1945 Leo leased the store to Lloyd Paxton and purchased a roller rink in nearby Galena. When Paxton's lease expired, Lora, then a widow, returned to manage the store as Lora Williams' AG Food Market. In 1971 Lora transferred ownership of the property to her daughter, Jane. Joe and Isabelle Eisler bought the business from Thelma Ball in 1973 and continue to operate it as a store and deli with nephew Scott Nelson (president of the Kansas Route 66 Association) as manager. Although Interstate 44 bypassed this area in 1961 the store continues to survive as a result of its strong local customer base and the current crop of Route 66 explorers.

BAXTER SPRINGS
c. 1940s

Baxter Springs was founded when John Baxter and his family settled there in 1849. The nearby mineral springs are said to have miraculous healing powers and were known to the Osage Indians who long made regular trips there. As white settlers arrived in the area word of the springs spread and their popularity exploded. To accommodate the visitors, John Baxter opened an inn and tavern called Baxter's Place, but he was brutally murdered in a land dispute in 1859.

Baxter Springs became known as the "First Cow Town in Kansas" when in 1867 the first herd of longhorns from Texas were driven there and sold to buyers who took the cattle to markets farther north. Baxter Springs gained a rough-and-tumble reputation and the moniker "The toughest town on earth." From 1867 to 1872, as the cattle trade prospered, gunfights and public hangings became commonplace. When rail lines were built into Texas, cattle no longer had to be driven north, and law and order were finally restored. Mining became the region's chief industry with the discovery of lead and zinc in nearby Picher, Oklahoma. As mining faded, so did the local economy. Through the years Baxter Springs has managed to survive and with the increased auto travel on Route 66 in the postwar period the town made a strong comeback. At one point Baxter Springs, because of its central location, was served by five large trucking companies and was used as an eight-state distribution point and maintenance depot for a major freight company.

BAXTER SPRINGS, KANSAS

OKLAHOMA

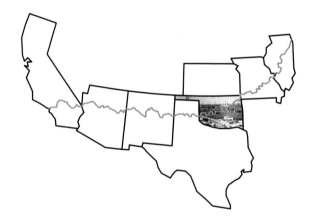

Route 66 was born in Oklahoma and its father was Cyrus Avery, a Tulsa businessman who became the state's first highway commissioner in 1913. After several years of lobbying for a national highway system, his hard work and perseverance paid off. In 1925 a letter from U.S. Secretary of Agriculture Howard Gore announcing the creation of a special board to "design and number a system of routes of interstate and national importance" arrived at his door. Gore asked Avery to act as a consultant to the American Association of State Highway Officials, which Avery persuaded to route the new highway through Oklahoma, Texas, New Mexico, Arizona, and into California. Prior to Avery's lobbying the new highway's path was to travel through Kansas and Colorado on its way to California. After much debate, Avery also convinced the board to settle on the number 66 for the new Chicago-to-Los Angeles highway.

In the early 1930s drought, dust storms, and the Great Depression triggered a mass migration of Texas, Arkansas, Kansas, and Colorado farmers to head for California's promised land. More than 200,000 of these Dust Bowl migrants fled through Oklahoma on Highway 66. John Steinbeck, in his Pulitzer Prize–winning novel, *The Grapes of Wrath,* forever immortalized to the world the plight of the Oklahoma farmer or "Okie." One can hardly forget the visual impact

characterized in John Ford's motion picture adaptation of three generations of the Joad family, tightly packed into their cut-down Hudson Super Six sedan, and struggling to cross the dry plains, desert, and mountains to reach California. "66 is the path of a people in flight, refugees from dust and shrinking land, from the thunder of tractors and shrinking ownership," wrote Steinbeck, "they come into 66 from the tributary side roads, from the wagon tracks and the rutted country roads. 66 is the mother road, the road of flight."

The Turner Turnpike (Interstate 44) between Tulsa and Oklahoma City, bypassed 100 miles of the Mother Road and was the first major bypass on the route. In 1957 the Will Rogers Turnpike opened between Tulsa and Miami, leaving another 100 miles of Route 66 to fend for itself. In 1975 the four-lane section of Route 66 from Sayre to Erick was the last section in Oklahoma to lose its U.S. 66 designation to I-40.

The pathway of Route 66 in Oklahoma covers approximately 400 miles and travels somewhat diagonally across the heart of the state, slicing through mining, agricultural, industrial, and oil regions. Although 66 went through countless changes over the years in Oklahoma, there are still more drivable "original" portions of Route 66 in that state than any other.

MIAMI
c. 1930s

Miami, Oklahoma, was established in 1891. That much is certain. How it got its name is a different matter. Some say Wayland C. Lykins, a cattle rancher attracted to the region's plentiful grazing land got the townsite approved, and on March 2, 1891, Miami became the first chartered town in "Indian Territory," named by Lykins for the local tribe. Others say Miami started out as a trading post called "Jimtown" because it was near the homes of four local farmers named Jim. In 1890 to expedite mail delivery, arrangements were made with one of the farmers, Jim Palmer, to establish a post office. The name Miami was chosen in honor of Palmer's wife, who was of Miami Indian blood. No matter which story you believe, remember: Miami is pronounced *my-am-uh* not *my-am-ee.*

In 1922, a unique stretch of roadway was built between Miami and Afton. When it came time to pave the 10 miles between the two cities, the highway commissioners from Craig and Ottawa counties found they had half the money necessary. Since the Federal Highway Commission required the road to be paved for the county to receive federal funds but did not specify width, engineer George Klein suggested they make the road a single lane 9 feet wide paved all the way. In 1937, this stretch was finally bypassed and became the last section of Route 66 in Oklahoma to be completely paved. Portions of this so-called "Ribbon Highway" or "Sidewalk Highway" can still be driven today.

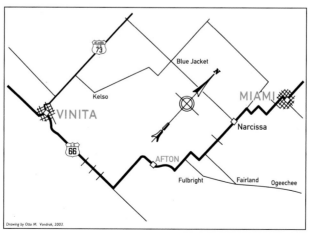

Drawing by Otto M. Vondrak, 2003.

AFTON
c. 1958

The small farming community of Afton was established in 1886 and given its name by railroad surveyor Anton Aires, who named the town after his daughter. Afton has many historic buildings lining its downtown area, including the old Palmer Hotel and the Rest Haven Motel. The Interstate bypass in 1957 and the decommissioning of Route 66 had a profoundly negative impact on Afton's economy. During the golden era of U.S. Highway 66, Afton was a thriving community with no less than six service stations and six motels lining its short stretch of Main Street. Today, there are very few survivors. On the outskirts of town stands the venerable Buffalo Ranch Trading Post, a landmark tourist stop built in 1953 by Russell and Aleene Kay with a budget of $5,000. The business eventually grew to include four buildings housing a trading post, western store, barbecue, dairy ranch, and a variety of livestock. The Buffalo Ranch closed its doors in 1997 when owner Aleene Albro (then remarried) died. The original buildings were torn down in 2002 and replaced with a new facility that includes a gas station and restaurant.

Afton is also home to Afton Station. From 1999 to the time of this writing, Laurel Kane has been restoring the 1930s-era gas station for use as a Route 66 visitors' center. Every attempt is being made to preserve the vintage flavor of the old service station, which originally sold Sunray DX petroleum products. An attached garage will serve as a museum for vintage automobiles.

MAIN STREET-HIGHWAY 66-AFTON, OKLA.

VINITA
c. 1939

Vinita, Oklahoma is not only the oldest incorporated town in Oklahoma, it is the second oldest town in the state. Vinita was established in 1871 and, like so many other towns in this part of Oklahoma, was primarily known as a railroad community. Originally known as Downingville, the name was later changed to honor Vinnie Ream, the local sculptress commissioned to carve the statue of Abraham Lincoln now located in the U.S. Capitol Building in Washington, D.C. Colonel Elias C. Boudinot, a Cherokee and one of the town site's first promoters, was responsible for the name change. Boudinot's father and 34 others were responsible for selling the Cherokee ancestral lands in the Southeast to the federal government.

The Trail of Tears mass migration that resulted in 1838 brought thousands of relocated Cherokees to the area.

Several historic buildings survive in Vinita, including the fully restored shopping district. Vinita is also home to Clanton's Café, built in 1927 and now being run by the fourth generation of Clantons. Hotel Vinita and the Spraker Service Station also served Route 66 during its heyday and were added to the National Register of Historic Places in 1995. In addition, Will Rogers went to the Willie Halsell Institute in Vinita, and it's said that he felt more at home there than at any other school he attended.

CATOOSA INDIAN TRADING POST, CATOOSA
c. 1955

Chief Wolfe Robe Hunt and his wife, Glenal, opened their first trading post out of their home in Tulsa in 1936. Not long after, they moved the shop to 11th Street (Route 66) in Tulsa. They were so successful selling Osage beadwork and Indian curios that they soon expanded the business to include Navajo jewelry and Acoma pottery, and opened a second store in Catoosa. When the Turner Turnpike bypassed Route 66, the business suffered and Chief Wolfe Robe Hunt and his wife moved the business to the newer location in Catoosa the following year. Chief Wolfe Robe Hunt pooled resources with his brother-in-law, Hugh Davis (builder of the famous Blue Whale across

the street), and the two entered business together, adding a gas station and café and changing the name to the Catoosa Indian Trading Post. Davis sold his portion of the business back to Chief Wolfe Hunt Robe in 1957. After the death of Chief Wolfe Robe Hunt the old trading post lay empty for many years until 1990, when Dave Jennings and his wife Pam bought the property and reopened the business as Arrowood's Trading Post. The gas pumps and café were long gone and the lack of business forced the trading post to close its doors in the late 1990s. The original building currently houses an auto repair shop.

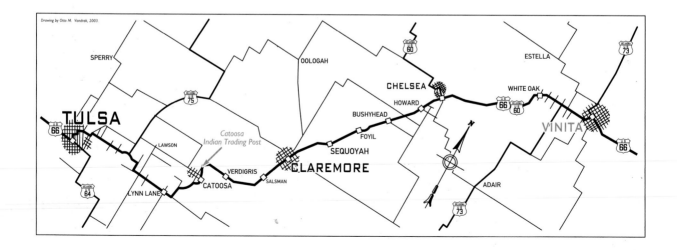

Drawing by Otto M. Vondrak, 2003

SHADY REST COURT, WEST TULSA
c. 1942

The Shady Rest Court is located in West Tulsa in what was once a suburb called Red Fork. Red Fork was responsible for putting Tulsa on the map as the "Oil Capital of the World" when a large oil field was found there in 1901. Maurice Colpitts, a Tulsa plumbing inspector, built the front-gable-style Shady Rest Cabins in 1936. Each of the 13 units was built around a 10x12 frame just large enough for a bed and two people. Unlike those at many motels, the Shady Rest carports were never converted to rooms, adding to the historic value and vintage feel.

During the glory days of Route 66 the Shady Rest Court offered "The best of accommodations for your money. Innerspring mattresses and air cooled cabins." The Shady Rest has seen four owners and only recently fell into a state of disrepair. The units are now quite run down and rented on a monthly basis. There is some hope, though, for the venerable old motor court. The original sign is being renovated and improvements and repairs are slowly being made to each cabin, according to current manager, Lorie Murphy. She hopes the new owners will realize and understand the historic importance of the Shady Rest Court and restore it to its original appearance, when tired motorists gladly stopped here for a "shady rest."

SHADY REST COURT
TULSA, OKLAHOMA

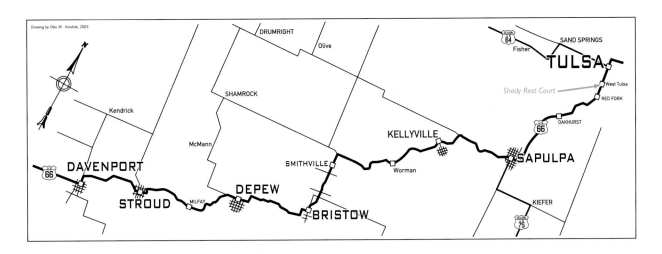

Drawing by Otto M. Vondrak, 2003.

VIEW FROM THE
CAPITOL BUILDING, OKLAHOMA CITY
c. 1935

Route 66 carried motorists directly in front of the Capitol Building in Oklahoma City, the only state capital on the entire route, via Lincoln Boulevard. Oklahoma City became the largest boomtown of the 1889 Land Rush when the region was opened for white settlement despite the promise of being "forever" set aside as "Indian Territory." On April 22 of that year, more than 10,000 people flocked to an area known as the Cherokee Strip between noon and sundown to stake claim to their land. Many of the settlers illegally camped out beforehand, hoping to get an advantage on the competition. These early birds were given the

name "Sooners," a nickname still applied to University of Oklahoma sports teams and the state nickname "The Sooner State." A second boom took place during the depression years when oil was struck in the area. By 1946, more than 1,000 oil derricks were located in and around the city, many of which still produce oil to this day. Most of the vintage Route 66 charm in Oklahoma City is long gone, the cafés, diners, classic service stations, and motor courts but a fond memory. But if you spend time and look hard enough, there are still remnants of the Mother Road waiting to be discovered in Oklahoma City.

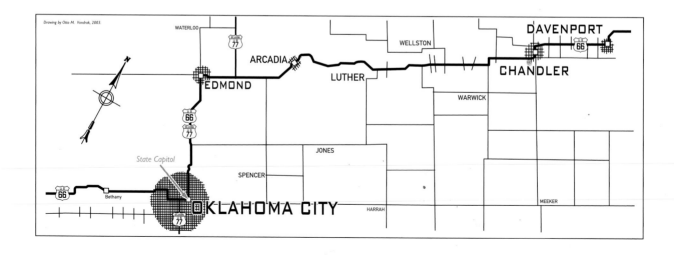

Drawing by Otto M. Vondrak, 2003.

HAMONS' COURT
(AKA LUCILLE'S), HYDRO
c. 1941

The original two-story building that eventually housed Hamons' Gas Station was built in 1927 by a man named Carl Ditmore of Hydro, Oklahoma. After a couple of years a five-unit motel was built behind the station. Carl and Lucille Hamons bought the Provine Station in 1941 and renamed it Hamons' Court. When construction of Interstate 40 in the area was completed in 1962, access to Hamons' Court was cut off and the couple closed the motel. Carl passed away in 1971. Lucille eventually changed the station's name to Lucille's, and in 1997 it was placed on the National Register of Historic Places (as the Provine Station). In 1999, Lucille was inducted in the Route 66 Hall of Fame at age of 84. The original Hamons' Court sign was shipped to the Smithsonian Institute in 2003.

Lucille passed away in August 2000; hundreds attended her funeral. Anyone would be hard-pressed to accurately describe Lucille, who was at once kind and generous, but also stubborn and forceful when fighting for something she believed in. Countless times she provided food to hungry travelers with no money or a free place to stay when their cars broke down. She fought heartily for an exit when the Interstate threatened to cut off her business. When the state told her they were trying to get rid of these small places along the highway, it only fueled her resolve. She lived on Route 66 for 59 years, serving and caring for thousands along the way. She truly earned the title "Mother of the Mother Road."

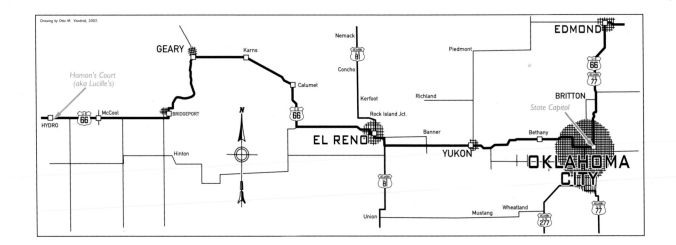

Drawing by Otto M. Vondrak, 2003.

COTTON BOLL MOTEL, CANUTE
c. 1960

The small community of Canute is home to one of the most photographed landmarks on all of Route 66. The Cotton Boll Motel is certainly not the oldest motel on the route, nor is it an architectural standout, but something about the classic red and white sign outlined in red and green neon attracts tourists from around the country. Woodrow and Viola Penick, both former cotton farmers, built the Cotton Boll in 1960, using the classic L-shape with parking in front of each unit. A central courtyard was replaced with a swimming pool in later years. The back of this postcard advertises, "16 units completely new and modern. Wall to wall carpets. Tile baths, free TV in rooms. Refrigerated Air-conditioning, baby cribs, laundry, complimentary coffee in rooms."

Business was "excellent," according to Viola, until 1970 when Interstate 40 bypassed Canute. Woodrow and Viola sold the motel in 1979. During the short oil boom in the early 1980s the Cotton Boll's new owners rented rooms to workers from nearby oil fields. In the mid-1990s the motel was purchased by Pat and Cheryl Webb, who turned the office and Room 1 into a private home. To area residents, the Cotton Boll's sign has become a symbol and a reminder of the days when America's Main Street rolled through town. While many of these locals feared the new owners would have the sign removed, the Webbs have no intention of bringing down the landmark. "This is a big part of their life," Pat says.

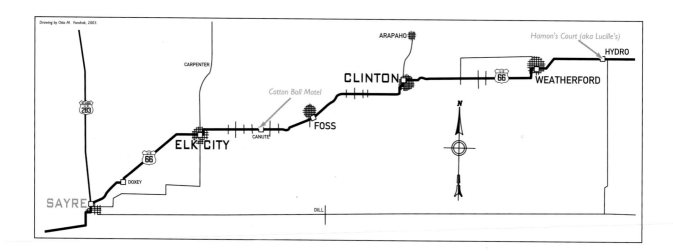

SAYRE
c. 1940

The Beckham County seat was named for Robert H. Sayre, a stockholder in the railroad that reached Sayre at its founding in 1901. The north fork of the Red River flows along the southern outskirts of the town, and at one time the area was developed into a public park that included several sandy beaches. The Beckham County Courthouse in this photograph appeared very briefly in John Ford's movie version of *The Grapes of Wrath*. Onetime heavyweight boxing champion of the world Jess Willard called Sayre home and ran a boarding house in town for many years.

In 1924, prior to the designation of U.S. Highway 66, a 2,600-foot-long timber bridge was constructed across the Red River to carry traffic on the newly designated State Highway 3. By 1926, the road carried the new 66 designation. With the increase of automobile traffic, the bridge needed fortification and in 1933 steel beams were incorporated. The revamped bridge remained in use until 1958 when a new bridge was opened on the new four-lane alignment. The remains of the original bridge, which burned in 1959, now sit on private property. Story has it that soon after the bridge burned and a barricade was constructed at the river bank, local high school kids would hang around the bridge site and frantically warn out-of-state drivers that "The Indians attacked and burned down the bridge. You'd better roll up your windows and head for the state line."

TEXAS

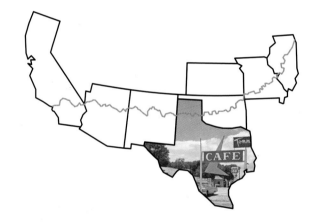

Route 66 crosses the pancake-like plains of the Texas panhandle, covering the 178 miles between Oklahoma and New Mexico. The panhandle is sometimes called the *Llano Estacado* or "Staked Plains," because early settlers in the area marked their routes by driving stakes into the ground. Kiowa and Comanche Indians roamed the region of Texas a mere 100 years ago.

People from all walks of life throughout the country saw Route 66 as a ticket to a new and better life "out West." During the late 1940s and into the 1950s families took to the road for their yearly vacations, often heading through Texas, which was fine as far as Texans were concerned. Route 66, which arrived in Texas in 1926, played an integral role in the economic growth of towns like Shamrock, McLean, Groom, Amarillo, Vega, and Adrain.

Early on, a journey through Texas on Route 66 was a rough, bumpy, and often hazardous ride. Because the Texas Highway Department gave priority to roads serving cities like Dallas, Houston, and San Antonio, conditions on 66 were generally subpar. One case in point was the dreaded "Jericho Gap," the portion stretching between McLean and Groom. After a rainfall many locals made extra cash by pulling stranded motorists out of the thick mud with teams of horses. In 1932 the section from McLean to Alanreed was bypassed and paved leaving about 18 miles of dirt from Alanreed to Groom. In 1933 construction finally began on a paved bypass there as well, but it wasn't until 1937 that the work was completed, making the stretch that paralleled the dreaded Jericho Gap one of the last sections on all of Route 66 to be paved.

During World War II military truck traffic took its toll on Route 66 in Texas, as it did in Missouri, and the surge of postwar automobile traffic further deteriorated the roadbed. Nevertheless, postwar families braved the road by the scores. Unlike its role in the 1920s and 1930s, Texas became a frontrunner in highway safety in the years following the war. Jack Rittenhouse, author of *A Guide Book to Highway 66* (1946), wrote when crossing the border from Oklahoma, "At once the road improves. Texas has wide splendid roads with excellent shoulders. There are many roadside parks throughout this part of the state." By 1954 Highway 66 was a modern four-lane highway from the Oklahoma border to just east of Groom, and from Amarillo west to Bushland. All of Route 66 in Texas was upgraded to four-lane status by 1960, with Interstate 40 designation from Shamrock to Conway. By 1966 the only two-lane section still in use was east of Vega to Glenrio at the New Mexico border. By the mid-1970s I-40 bypassed most Texas towns, with the exceptions of McLean and Groom. Amarillo, the largest Route 66 city in Texas, was completely bypassed in 1968. Groom survived the interstate until 1980, and McLean, one of the last holdouts along the entire route, did not succumb to I-40 until 1984.

Many of the towns that once enjoyed the abundance of postwar tourist travel have suffered the same sad fate as the road itself. During the road's heyday a trip west through Texas would include a multitude of "tourist traps." Live rattlesnake pits and great gas prices were but a few of the marketing ploys designed to convince travelers to stop. Some still exist but most have gone the way of the dial telephone. One holdover is the Big Texan Steak Ranch in Amarillo, which has a standing offer: finish their 72-ounce steak with all of the fixins' in one hour, and the meal is free.

U DROP INN, SHAMROCK
c. 1942

The art deco U Drop Inn at the intersection of Route 66 and U.S Highway 83 was built in 1936 from plans scratched out in the dirt by John Nunn with an old nail. So the story goes. The main building was built of brick with green and gold glazed tile accents, while the towers are wood-framed and covered with stucco. A contest to name the café was won by a local 10-year-old who pocketed $5 in the process. As the only café for about a 100-mile radius, the U Drop Inn enjoyed a brisk business.

Around 1937 the space next to the café that served as a store was transformed into a dining room and ballroom. Original proprietors John and Bebe Nunn sold the café after a few years, only to repurchase it in 1950 and change its name to Nunn's Café. John died in 1957, and in 1960 Bebe sold the business to Grace Brunner, who changed the name once again. The rechristened Tower Café also served as Shamrock's Greyhound bus station and fed hundreds of travelers daily. After a few more ownership changes, the building was purchased in the early 1980s by the son of the original financier, James Tindal Jr., who had the building repainted to its original color and restored the U Drop Inn moniker. Today the U Drop Inn is an information center created with a $1.7 million federal restoration grant.

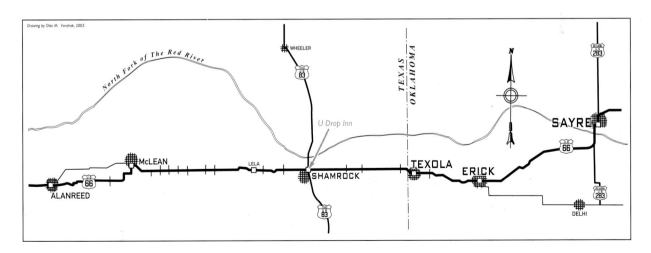

AMARILLO
c. 1958

In 1887 the Fort Worth & Denver City Railway was building across the Texas panhandle when it established a tent city, known as "Ragtown," along an area creek. A permanent townsite was subsequently argued over and voted on. On August 30, 1887, the site proposed by local rancher Colonel James T. Berry was selected. Originally called Oneida, it was soon changed to Amarillo (Spanish for "yellow"), some say for the color of the soil along the creek banks, others for the region's abundant yellow wildflowers. By 1893 it was said that Amarillo's population was "between 500-600 humans and 50,000 head of cattle."

In the early days, Route 66 entered Amarillo from the east via Northeast 8th Street (now Amarillo Boulevard) and continued just north of downtown, where it took a 90-degree turn south on Fillmore Street. The highway traveled through downtown, west on 6th Street, and on through San Jacinto Heights, veering off to 9th Street and eventually out of the city. Route 66 on 8th Street at the eastern end of town was considered "motel row," where dozens of tourist courts lined the street with colorful names like the Cowboy Motel, Cactus Motel, Silver Spur, Longhorn, and Wagon Wheel. By 1953 traffic was rerouted west on Amarillo Boulevard past Fillmore Street to relieve the traffic snarl downtown. The San Jacinto portion was paved in brick in 1927, making it the first paved highway in Amarillo. In 1968 Interstate 40 opened to traffic, bypassing the city and motel row.

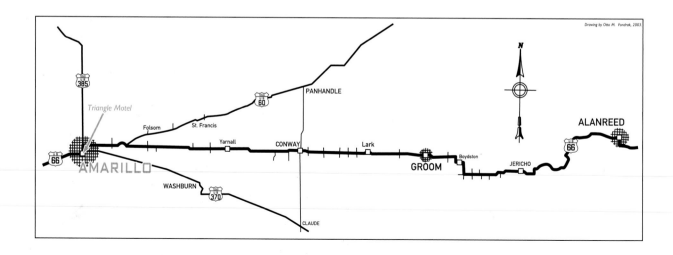

Drawing by Otto M. Vondrak, 2003.

TRIANGLE MOTEL, AMARILLO
c. 1949

S. M. Clayton was onetime mayor of Borger, Texas, known among some as "the wickedest town in the West." After his retirement from politics he and his wife Cora moved to Amarillo and built the Triangle Motel complex on the eastern edge of town, naming it for its wedge-shaped lot created by the intersection of Route 66 and Highway 60. The streamline moderne motel was designed with two parallel brick buildings that faced each other, separated by a courtyard in the center. Each building housed six rooms and a convenient, closed-in two-car garage between every two rooms.

During its heyday, the Triangle catered to the families and dependants of servicemen stationed at the nearby air force base.

In the late 1950s the Strategic Air Command opened the 4128th Strategic Wing at the base and extended its runways to accommodate the newer and bigger jets. Highway 60 was closed as a result. In 1968 the motel suffered two major setbacks with the deactivation of the air base and the completion of the Interstate bypass around Amarillo. Slowly, the motel fell into a state of disrepair. In 1977 Vaughn and Ramona Price bought the property and used the empty buildings mostly for storage. The structure that once housed the restaurant has since been opened and now serves as a bar and local hangout.

VEGA MOTEL, VEGA
c. 1960

In the small town of Vega, 40 miles west of Amarillo, sits the Vega Motel at the crossroads of old Route 66 and U.S. 385. E. M. and Josephine Pancoast built the 20-unit motel in the early 1940s, and it is a prime example of the era's U-shaped motor courts with a fully covered garage for each unit and a central courtyard. The property was sold to Ethridge Betts in the early 1970s, and the current owners, Harold and Tresa Whaley, bought the motel in 1988. Tresa sews the bedspreads and curtains used in the rooms. Many of the rooms have been remodeled, but Tresa says they are careful not to ruin the old charm and style. "Love, sweat and tears have gone into this place,"

says Tresa. When a blizzard left guests snowbound in 1991, Tresa's brother Manuel and daughter Joanna trekked to the grocery store in a four-wheel-drive vehicle. Tresa and Joanna then fixed a traditional Thanksgiving dinner for her family and stranded guests.

Unlike many owners of motels from this era, the Whaleys have not converted the garages to rooms, thus maintaining the 1940s styling. At the time of this writing, paperwork had begun to add the motel to the National Register of Historic Places. Tresa speaks fondly of the fact that in the early 1990s country music star Vince Gill shot the video for his song "I Never Knew Lonely" in Room 21.

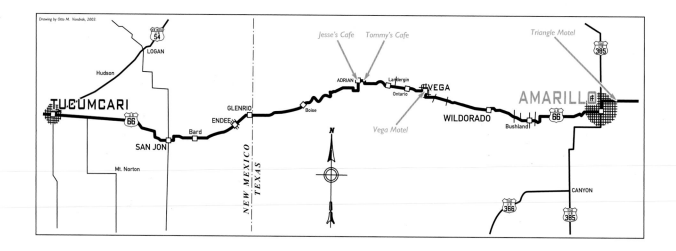

Drawing by Otto M. Vondrak, 2003.

TOMMY'S CAFÉ, ADRIAN
c. 1962

Manuel Loveless built the Kozy Kottage Kamp in Adrian in the early 1940s. The Kamp's service station and café were destroyed by fire in December 1947, but the Loveless family continued renting cabins under the name Adrian Court. The property where the service station and café once stood was sold to the Harris family. Bob Harris, who had worked at the Kozy Kottage Kamp before World War II, returned after the war with the idea of building a café on the newly acquired property. Harris wanted to design the café in a way that would compel motorists to stop. The nearby U.S. Army Air Force bases were selling surplus military items, including a control tower. Harris bought the tower, moved it to his property, and proceeded to build his café around it. The eatery was christened the Bent Door Café for the canted door that accommodated its slanting walls.

Harris left Adrian and his mother to operate the café, and in 1950 Loveless leased the restaurant. In the late 1960s the Interstate bypassed Adrian and the steady flow of traffic slowed to a trickle. In 1970 the onetime 24-hour café and service station closed their doors. They sat empty for three decades until Harris returned for a visit and heard the café was to be condemned. He repurchased the property and set a reopening for September 9, 1995, but it wasn't to be. On September 9 the fryers and ovens sat empty and cold. The café has remained closed since.

JESSE'S CAFÉ, ADRIAN
c. 1965

In 1956 Dub Edmonds and former Navy cook Jesse Fincher opened Jesse's Café in "an old building a cowboy built of cinder blocks," recalls Edmonds. A gas station located alongside the café was also part of their enterprise, which at one time was a one-room, dirt-floor café called Zella's. In 1965 a second story A-frame apartment was added above the café and a new canopy was built over the pumps. The apartment burned twice and was not rebuilt after the second fire. Jesse's Café was so successful that a second restaurant, Jesse's #2, went up in nearby Wilderado about 30 miles east of Adrian. Edmonds and Fincher ran both locations until 1976 when they sold the Adrian location to Terry and Peggy Crietz, who

changed the name to Peggy's. The business was later sold again and became known as Rachel's.

Fincher's pies became famous in Adrian. Dub remembers, "He would bake pies and set them on the counter and most of them were sold before they got cold." Fincher passed away in 1989, leaving business matters to Edmonds, who sold the Wilderado location in 1991. Fran Hauser bought the Adrian location in 1990 and changed the name to the Adrian Café. Around 1995 she learned that Adrian was the mid-point on Route 66 and changed the name to the Mid-Point Café. Hauser continues the fine tradition of good food, friendly service, and delicious homemade pies begun in 1956.

NEW MEXICO

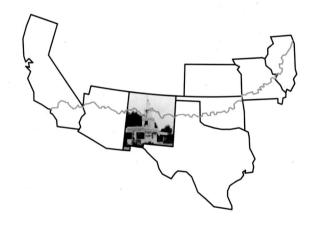

New Mexico was only 14 years old when Route 66 was created. The original 506-mile alignment through the state traversed many difficult obstacles, including deserts, snake-like canyons, and treacherous hills. Often the route utilized portions of the century-old Santa Fe Trail and the 300-year-old Camino Réal. The original alignment between Albuquerque and Santa Fe was considered the most treacherous and included the feared La Bajada Hill (Spanish for "the descent"). From 1926 to 1932 the hill provided early motorists with a multitude of challenges, including an average 6 percent grade and 20 switchbacks in 1.4 miles. Prior to the addition of fuel pumps in automobiles, motorists often climbed the hill in reverse to keep fuel flowing to gravity-fed carburetors. Descending La Bajada presented its own dangers. Early brake pads were often made of cloth and not very durable—riding one's brakes down the grade often set the pads on fire. At the top of the hill the State Highway Department posted a warning sign that read, "La Bajada Hill – Warning – Safe Speed 10 Mile – Watch Sharp Curves – This Road Is Not Fool Proof But Safe For A Sane Driver – Use Low Gear."

As automobiles gained popularity, many of the older paths traveled by Highway 66 quickly became obsolete. New Mexico saw its fair share of realignments, none as dramatic as that which took place in 1926. Around that time, Arthur T. Hannet was losing his bid for reelection as governor in a closely fought race. Feeling betrayed by his own political party and frustrated with state politics Hannet decided to avenge his loss by building a highway that would bypass the state capital. Governor-elect Richard Dillon would be sworn in in less than two months, so Hannet had little time to act. He called on state highway engineer E. B. Bail to begin a road-building project to start 6 miles west of Santa Rosa and head straight into Albuquerque. At the time, Highway 66 through New Mexico ran from Tucumcari to Santa Rosa, then to Romeroville, Glorieta, Santa Fe, and Albuquerque. Hannet's road would shorten the route to Albuquerque by about 89 miles and bypass Santa Fe's business community and politicians. By the time crews and equipment were secured, only 31 days remained to build 69 miles of roadway.

Angry citizens on Highway 66 to the north and Highway 60 to the south often sabotaged equipment, afraid of the economic impact of the new route. Vandalism, along with bitterly cold weather, slowed progress, but work forged ahead. Bail even brought the men blankets so they could sleep close to the machinery and protect it from further damage. Although the men worked non-stop, the new road was not quite finished by January 1. Dillon, immediately after taking oath on January 1, sent a representative to halt the construction. Bad weather kept him from arriving until January 3, however, by which time the road was completed. Hannet had his revenge. His road was originally designated New Mexico 6, paved by 1937, and redesignated as Highway 66 that same year.

The last segment of Route 66 in New Mexico was bypassed in 1981, four years before the entire route was officially decommissioned. In 1994 the surviving sections of Route 66 in New Mexico were designated as State Scenic Byways and in 2000 were recognized as National Scenic Byways.

TUCUMCARI
c. 1957

Tucumcari (pronounced *too-come-carry*) was first christened Six Gun Siding, but in 1902 citizens agreed that a more "respectful" name was needed, so they named it after a nearby mountain. Legend has it that a chief ordered two competing braves to the top of the mountain to fight to the death for the honor of marrying his daughter, Kari. Her lover, Tocom, lost the battle and in a violent rage she killed the victorious brave. Filled with anguish, she then sunk Tocom's knife into her own heart. Upon seeing what had transpired, the chief took the knife and plunged it into his own heart. Use your imagination, adjust the spelling a little, and voila.

During the halcyon days of Route 66, the indelible words "Tucumcari Tonight! 2,000 Motel Rooms" were splattered across billboards from Oklahoma City to California. Tucumcari was known as the town that was "two blocks wide and two miles long," for the concentration of motels, service stations, trading posts, and cafés along Route 66 through town. In the early days, however, Route 66 from the Texas border to Tucumcari was not well maintained and extremely narrow. Old timers would remark that you had "six inches and a cigarette paper between you and death on 66." Interstate 40 bypassed Tucumcari in 1980, but the town managed to survive. There may be fewer motel rooms these days, but the main drag is still filled with historic Route 66 motels, cafés, trading posts, and a legend or two for good measure.

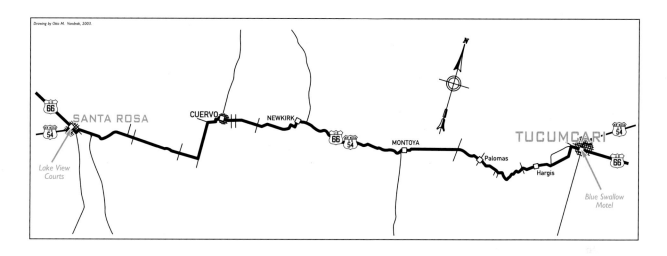

Drawing by Otto M. Vondrak, 2003.

BLUE SWALLOW COURT, TUCUMCARI, NEW MEXICO

In the City, East on U. S. Highway 66

BLUE SWALLOW COURT, TUCUMCARI
c. 1941

Since the early 1940s, the Blue Swallow has been a favorite haven among weary travelers. W. A. Huggins began construction on this truly classic motor court in 1939 and opened for business in 1941. The archetypal 1930s design features 13 units laid out in an L-shape with individual garages for each unit. The office sits prominently in the center. Ownership changed hands a few times over the years until 1958 when Floyd Redman purchased the property and gave it to his fiancée as an engagement gift. Lillian Redman owned and operated the motel for almost 40 years until age and the high cost of upkeep took their toll.

Slowly, the motel was headed downhill from lack of maintenance and Redman was forced to put it up for sale. With no prospective buyers it seemed another Route 66 icon was about to fade away. Fortunately, Dale and Linda Bakke saw an ad in a Denver newspaper listing the Blue Swallow for sale and, looking for a change of scenery, purchased the property. On March 13, 1998, substantial restoration efforts began. Unit by unit, room by room, and fixture by fixture, the classic Blue Swallow was lifted from the brink of extinction. Lillian Redman passed away in February of 1999 but no doubt would smile as once again the Blue Swallow proudly serves tired travelers.

SANTA ROSA
c. 1958

Santa Rosa, was founded in 1865 when rancher Don Celso Baca, drawn by the abundance of water, arrived and became "lord of the region" under the old custom of range domain. He named the new settlement after his wife and Saint Rose of Lima, the first canonized saint of the so-called New World. The coming of the railroad on Christmas Day 1901 turned the sleepy settlement into a vital transportation and service hub. Ironically, water, which attracted the railroad, was also the reason that industry fled Santa Rosa: the water was so high in mineral content it left gypsum deposits in steam engines, ruining the locomotives. With the departure of the railroad, Santa Rosa reverted to the sleepy town it once was.

When Highway 66 was routed through in 1926, Santa Rosa became an important stop. At one time, as many as 60 service stations, 20 motels, and 15 restaurants lined its main thoroughfare. The famous Blue Hole, located on one of Route 66's early alignments through town, is a natural, bell-shaped pool over 80 feet deep with amazing clarity and a constant water temperature of 64 degrees Fahrenheit. Scuba divers from around the country enjoy its unique blue waters. During the Dust Bowl era, the Blue Hole and the surrounding area served as a campground for thousands of migrants.

LAKE VIEW COURTS, SANTA ROSA
c. 1946

The Lake View Courts were built in 1941 and consisted of 10 units with covered garage parking for four of the rooms. A station serving Conoco gas was also part of the original structure. The motel operated as a successful business for 20 years until the early 1960s when the owner allowed it to fall into a state of disrepair. In the mid-1960s Canuto Sanchez Jr. purchased the property with the intent of tearing the motel down and erecting a new modern Ramada Inn in its place. Canuto decided against the new motel when news that the impending Interstate would eventually bypass Santa Rosa was confirmed. He opted to spruce up the existing motel with some fresh paint and to furnish the rooms with new beds and furniture. Along with the new look came a new name and the Lake View Courts were changed to the Plains Motel. The newly remodeled inn and newly added Amoco gas station became favorite stops in town until November 1972 when the Interstate was completed, leaving Santa Rosa high and dry. The motel closed in April 1973 and has been used for storage for the past 30 years. The service station reopened in 1975 under the Exxon banner and remained open until 1980.

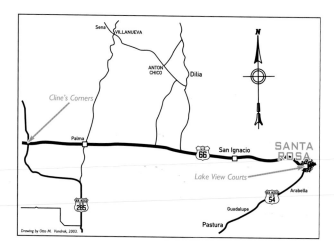

Drawing by Otto M. Vondrak, 2003.

CLINE'S CORNERS
c. 1958

After several failed business ventures in New Mexico and Arkansas, Roy Cline and his son Roy Jr. in 1934 leased 80 acres where Highways 6 and 2 intersected and built a small café and Conoco station. In 1937 the highways were paved and relocated, so Roy had the buildings jacked up and moved to the new intersection, Highway 2 now being U.S. Highway 285 and Highway 6 becoming Route 66. During the early years, things were tough going. At night Roy turned on the lights only when a car approached. If they stopped he left them on; if they passed, he turned them off and waited for another car.

Eventually, Cline's Corners became Roy's most lucrative venture. He sold the business in 1939 and moved, but eventually returned to New Mexico and opened another Route 66 service station, which he owned and operated until 1963. Located 77 miles east of Albuquerque, the Flying C Ranch at first consisted of a gas station, garage, and café. Today, it is a fully modern facility known as Bowlin's Flying C Ranch, and includes a gas station, curio shop, and Dairy Queen. After Roy sold Cline's Corners, it became so large that in 1964 a post office was added and homes were built behind the business to provide living quarters for most of its 48 employees. Over the years Cline's Corners became a Route 66 landmark and, later, a favorite stop on Interstate 40 that today serves an estimated 15 million customers each year.

LONGHORN RANCH, MORIARTY
c. 1948

"Where the West Stops to Rest" was the catchy advertising slogan of the Longhorn Ranch. Located 45 miles east of Albuquerque, the Longhorn sat along Route 66 on the barren desert landscape of eastern New Mexico, tempting first-time travelers out West to stop and rest a spell. "Captain Eric" Erikson, a former police officer from back East, opened the Longhorn with only a counter and a few stools. Eventually the tiny café was expanded to include a restaurant, coffee shop, cocktail lounge, motel, curio shop, and full-service garage. The storefronts were set up to look like the Western towns one would see in the movies, with a pair of totem poles guarding the curio shop.

The Longhorn was the first taste of the Old West for many motorists traveling along Route 66. Among the many attractions at the ranch, riding the bright red stagecoach, pulled by four paint horses with Hondo the Cowboy at the reins, was probably the most popular. Afterward, kids could have their picture taken with Hondo and the stagecoach. The Longhorn Ranch also kept several exotic animals on display for tourists to enjoy, including oxen, a large Brahma bull, buffalo, and a special longhorn steer named "Babe." The Longhorn Ranch became a landmark institution on Route 66, and at its height of popularity hosted thousands of tourists each day. Today, only ruins and memories remain of one of the most glamorous tourist attractions on Route 66.

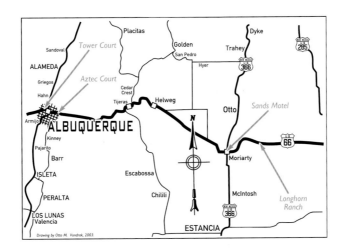

SANDS MOTEL, MORIARTY
c. 1954

A man today remembered as Mr. Simms built the Sands Motel in 1954 to consist of six rooms with enclosed garages alongside each room. As with many Route 66 motor courts, the garages were eventually converted to four rooms. Simms owned the motel for a very short time, selling the property in 1955. In 1968, J. C. Alderson, a plumber by trade, bought the property and eventually expanded the room total to 18 by adding two trailers out back for extra rooms. A trucking company with a regular route through Moriarty used the trailer rooms.

"We never had much trouble around here except one day around 1972," recalls Alderson's son, Jace. "One morning we went in to clean one of the rooms that was rented by a couple the night before and found the sheets, pillowcases, blankets, towels, and TV missing. That night our next-door neighbor, who owned a wrecker service, pulled in with a wrecked car. I asked what happened and he said, 'Someone stole [the] car last night . . . if you look in the backseat I think that there are some things in there that belong to you.' Sure enough, all of our missing items were in the backseat. It turns out the couple was on the run and wanted by the FBI." The Aldersons rented nightly rooms until they sold the property in 2001. At the time of this writing, the motel was being remodeled for use as storefronts.

AZTEC COURT, ALBUQUERQUE
c. 1941

In 1931 Guy and May Fargo built the Aztec Court at an estimated cost of $8,000 at 3821 Central Avenue on the east side of Albuquerque. "Innerspring mattresses, furnace heat and moderate rates" were some of the advertised amenities. In 1937 Route 66 was relocated to New Mexico 6, a straight shot from Santa Rosa to Albuquerque, giving Central Avenue a major increase in traffic. Tourist-based businesses began popping up all along the street, as a steady stream of automobiles flowed down Route 66, especially in the summer months. Guy passed away in 1942 but May continued to operate the motel until she sold it in 1944. Two years later the property was again sold to a pair of couples, William and Emma Geck and Wesley and Bertha Meyer, who owned and operated the motel until the early 1950s. Later in the decade the name was changed several more times through the course of eight ownership changes. In 1958 Floyd and Evelyn Lewis bought the property and changed the name to Aztec Motel, which remains in use today. The Aztec passed through a few more hands between 1962 and 1992, when Mohamed and Shokey Natha bought the property. After 64 years and 14 ownership changes, the oldest continuously operated auto court on New Mexico's Route 66 was entered into the National Register of Historic Places in 1993.

TOWER COURT, ALBUQUERQUE
c. 1939

The Tower Court was built by Ben F. Shear in 1939, just two years after the relocation of Route 66 through Albuquerque via Central Avenue. The mostly single-story motel was constructed using the classic U-shape layout and utilizes a distinctively streamline moderne architectural style. Typical of auto court design during the 1930s, pull-in garages were located alongside each unit, with all but one still in use today. The unusual rear wing of the motel contains a second story consisting of two units mirroring the lower units. Originally, a 30-foot stepped tower containing the motel office was located at the front of the property, accentuating the unique design of the motel. The tower has since been removed. The motel was originally built containing 15 units and remained that way with no additions over its lifetime. The Tower Court was a member of the United Auto Courts and was a recommended stop by AAA. Eventually, to keep up with the times, the "Court" was dropped and the name was changed to the Tower Motel. Relatively unchanged since 1939, the Tower Motel is one of the oldest remaining tourist courts along Albuquerque's Central Avenue/Route 66 commercial strip. It is also a classic example of auto courts built prior to World War II. The Tower Motel no longer serves nightly guests but is an apartment building renting units by the month. On November 22, 1993, it was added to the National Register of Historic Places.

JOHNNIES CAFÉ, THOREAU
C. LATE 1920s

At the time of its construction, both Johnnies and Highway 66, then a primitive dirt path, were located on the north side of the tracks in Thoreau (pronounced *thuh-roo*). In February 1936, founders Johnnie and Helen Maich sold the business to John and Anna Radosevich. John was the cook and his wife Anna did a little bit of everything, including waiting tables. The small café was only 20x40 and consisted of a counter with a couple of stools and four tables. In its early years, the food was prepared on a Coleman wood stove and dishes were washed with water heated by a wood fire. A one-cylinder diesel generator was pressed into service to supply electricity for lights during the evening hours. Shortly after John and Anna purchased the café, Route 66 was rerouted to the south side of the tracks. Johnnies itself was moved, building and all, to its current location along side the new alignment in 1947. In 1949 an addition was made to the building's east side, and in the early 1950s another section was built on to the west side. Today, the western addition is an off-sale liquor store. Johnnies was well known in the area for serving outstanding chili and thick steaks. "People would drive from Gallup just for the chili," says John Radosevich, whose family still owns the building.

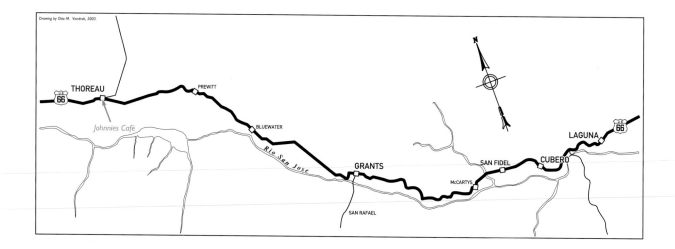

Drawing by Otto M. Vondrak, 2003.

JOHNNIES CAFE, THOREAU, N. MEX.
GOOD EATS
Reasonable Prices   **Tourist Headquarters**
U. S. HIGHWAY 66

Mileage from Johnnies Cafe

WEST TO		EAST TO	
Continental Divide	5	Grants	31
Gallup, N. Mexico	32	Laguna	65
Painted Desert	106	Los Lunas	116
Petrified Forest	118	Albuquerque	139
Holbrook, Ariz.	134	Domingo	176
Winslow	167	Santa Fe	203
Flagstaff	230	Las Vegas	277
Maine	250	Trinidad, Colo.	418
Grand Canyon	315	**NORTH TO**	
Williams	266	Crown Point	28
Needles, Cal.	470	Chaco Canyon	60
Los Angeles	770	**SOUTH TO**	
		Albuquerque	139
		El Paso	444

LOG CABIN LODGE, GALLUP
c. 1952

Tony and Francis Leone built the Log Cabin Lodge in 1937. Originally, it consisted of six log cabins and a single-story office building. A fireplace in each cabin provided ambience and heat during the cold winter nights. "Every day, each cabin was set up with a supply of paper and logs for an evening fire" says Lois Berger, daughter of Tony and Francis. Each cabin also featured a kitchenette, all of which were eventually eliminated because of the added time required to clean up after guests. Beds replaced the kitchen appliances, adding extra sleeping space to each cabin. Navajo rugs and taxidermy filled the roomy lobby that also offered a large central fireplace.

During the 1940s and 1950s the Log Cabin Lodge was part of the Best Western chain and two double log cabins were added, as well as a whole new wing built in an adobe style with side-by-side rooms and attached garages. The property was sold around 1959, but the new owner was unable to keep up with the mortgage payments and the lodge reverted back to the Leones. Multiple owners followed, but time took its toll on the landmark. Maintenance and upkeep over the years were sorely lacking and the Log Cabin Lodge eventually fell into a dismal state of disrepair. The Log Cabin Lodge was listed on the National Register of Historic Places in 1993. The last guest checked out sometime in the mid-1990s and it has remained vacant ever since.

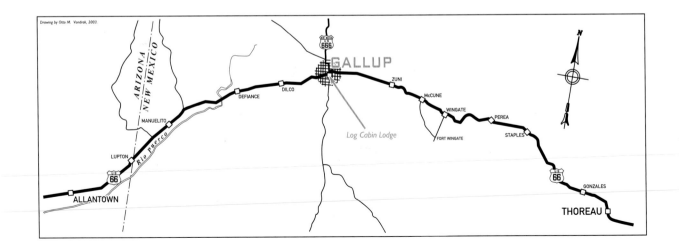

Drawing by Otto M. Vondrak, 2003.

114

LOG CABIN LODGE
GALLUP, NEW MEXICO

U. S. Highway 66, ¼ Mile West of Business Center

ARIZONA

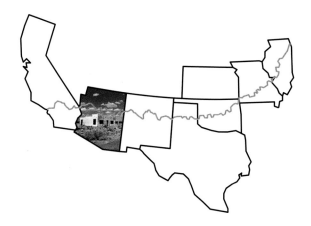

When U.S. Highway 66 was designated in 1926, existing roads, variations of Beale's Wagon Road and other old trails, were stitched together from town to town to form the fledgling highway. Highway 66 entered Arizona from the east via Lupton and continued through Holbrook, Winslow, Winona, Flagstaff, Williams, Ash Fork, Seligman, Peach Springs, Kingman, Oatman, and finally Topock.

U.S. Highway 66 originally spanned 385 miles across northern Arizona, and, as in other states, a vast majority of the road was dirt and poorly maintained. As traffic grew, motels, cafés, and service stations sprang up to accommodate travelers, and each town stretched its city limits as more and more businesses vied for the tourist dollar. By 1934 most of the Mother Road in Arizona was paved. Near the end of 1937 paving was complete across Arizona, which also saw its fair share of alignment changes over the years. In 1953 the perilous hairpin path from Kingman to Oatman over Sitgreaves Pass was eliminated in favor of a straighter route bypassing Oatman via Yucca on its way to Topock. In the May 1955 issue of *Arizona Highways* it was reported that 2,999 vehicles used Route 66 in Arizona every day, or 1,094,635 vehicles per year, of which 73 percent were from out of state. In 1955, the magazine added, the total length of Route 66 through Arizona was 376 miles, with 174.8 being constructed to the minimum 40-foot width, the Interstate standard.

Construction of Interstate 40 in Arizona was full speed ahead in the 1960s, and by 1969 most rural sections of Route 66 were upgraded or replaced. The first city to be bypassed was Flagstaff in 1968, but construction of other city bypasses moved at a much slower rate and it wasn't until 1978 that the next city, Winslow, saw a bypass. That same year the Interstate opened from Seligman to Kingman, leaving numerous small towns in an economic nosedive, including Peach Springs, which holds the dubious honor of being bypassed by 36 miles, the most of any city on the route. Holbrook, Joseph City, Ash Fork, and Kingman were all bypassed in 1981, but it wasn't until October 13, 1984, that Williams became the last city on the entire route to be bypassed.

Route 66 across Arizona is a study in scenic contrasts as one travels west from the wide-open spaces of the eastern high desert on a gradual climb through the beautiful, dense pine forests east of Flagstaff to Williams. From Williams, at an elevation of 7,000 feet, 66 drops abruptly down Ash Fork Hill to just over 5,000 feet in about 6 miles. From Ash Fork, the route travels west past Seligman, where the landscape changes again and the treeless expanse of the Aubrey Valley comes into view. From there, the road gradually descends over rolling hills to Kingman at 3,328 feet, eventually reaching the low desert terrain of Topock and the Colorado River, where the elevation is a mere 507 feet above sea level. Much of the Mother Road in Arizona lies directly beneath the path of Interstate 40. Nevertheless, there are still many sections of the old road that survive and are well worth the time to explore them.

PAINTED DESERT
TRADING POST, NAVAJO
c. 1942

Imagine the loneliest, most sun-baked desert expanse conceivable, where a single lizard might be the only living thing—other than yourself—for miles. There, right smack dab in the middle of lonely, you will find the Painted Desert Trading Post. Dotch and Alberta Windsor opened the Painted Desert Trading Post in the early 1940s, selling Indian curios, cold drinks, and sandwiches, as well as gasoline from gravity pumps. The trading post had no telephone, so calls were placed at the Painted Desert Park several miles to the west. Appliances ran on electricity generated by a windmill. The Windsors operated the post together until their marriage ended around 1950. Joy Nevin, who ran a veterinary supply business in Holbrook, Arizona,

met Dotch at the trading post during a business trip and the couple married, with Joy giving birth to a daughter in 1952. Dotch and Joy operated the trading post together until they divorced in 1956.

The section of Route 66 that ran past the business was relocated, widened, and designated Interstate 40 in the late 1950s, and the trading post has sat empty and abandoned ever since. Joy went on to become a leading figure in nearby Holbrook, where a street is named in her honor. Dotch died in October 1964, but the skeletal remains of the Painted Desert Trading Post still sit alongside the abandoned roadway, slowly being reclaimed by the desert that once gave it life.

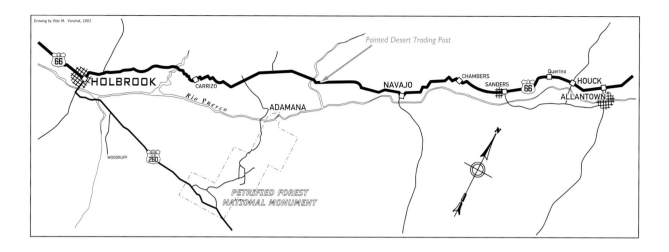

Drawing by Otto M. Vondrak, 2003.

Painted Desert Trading Post

ELLA'S FRONTIER
TRADING POST, JOSEPH CITY
c. 1950s

Ella's Frontier Trading Post sits on an abandoned section of Route 66 just outside the western edge of Joseph City. The business was owned and operated by Ella Blackwell, who purchased the property (previously called the Last Frontier Trading Post) in 1955 after divorcing her second husband. A former student at the Julliard School, Ella kept a piano in the store, which she claimed was established in 1873, making it the oldest such establishment on Route 66. Ella, however, was considered quite eccentric among locals, many of whom doubted her claim. Nevertheless, Ella's Frontier was in every way a classic tourist stop. Most of the things sold there—feather headdresses, moccasins, rubber snakes—would be considered mere souvenirs to adults, but treasures to kids traveling out West with their folks. Theo Hunsaker, the executor of Ella's estate, claims, "She had acquaintances all over the world; people who had stopped there would stay in touch with her." When she died in 1984, Hunsaker found duffel bags full of her correspondence.

In 1969, Interstate 40 bypassed Ella's, marking the beginning of the end for the longstanding roadside tourist stop. Standing on the dead-end road that once carried hundreds of automobiles each day with travelers gazing at Ella's Frontier and dreaming of the cold soda in the machine door or the large tomahawk under the counter glass, you get the feeling of being in a life-size, historical diorama—a living museum piece complete with a barely audible Mozart sonata drifting through the ruins.

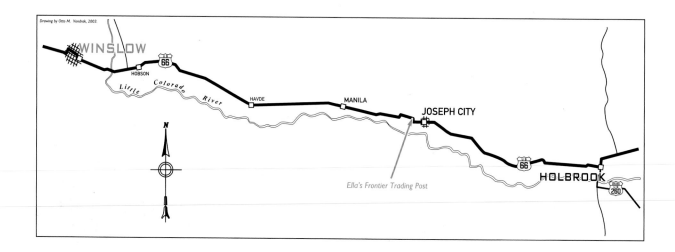

Ella's Frontier Trading Post

WINSLOW
c. 1938

"Standin' on a corner in Winslow, Arizona/Such a fine sight to see." The popular Eagles song of the early 1970s immortalized the corner of Second Street and Kingsley in downtown Winslow. Second Street carried Route 66 until 1951, when the ever-increasing stream of cars made it necessary to divide the flow of traffic through town. Second Street was assigned one-way traffic eastbound, and Third Street carried westbound travelers. Unfortunately, this grizzled railroad town fell on hard times when Interstate 40 bypassed it in the late 1960s and most businesses moved out nearer to the Interstate, leaving downtown Winslow looking somewhat like a ghost town.

Signs along this portion of the route commemorate the stretch as being part of the old Beale's Wagon Road; other markers point out the use of this trail by Mormon immigrants in the 1870s. Wayne L. Troutner's Store for Men was the clothier of choice for locals and lonely travelers wanting to spruce up before "standin' on a corner" and hoping to be noticed by that special gal passing by in a "flatbed Ford." Like so many roadside business owners along Route 66, Troutner was innovative when it came to roadside advertising, and created quite a stir when he placed billboards depicting a vivacious young cowgirl along Route 66 and other highways out West. The billboards became popular worldwide with sightings reported as far away as Paris and Guam.

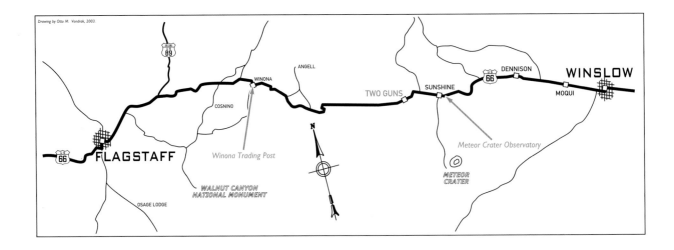

Drawing by Otto M. Vondrak, 2003.

Winona Trading Post

Meteor Crater Observatory

METEOR CRATER OBSERVATORY, WEST OF WINSLOW
c. 1946

Harry and Hope Locke began work on the impressive, castle-like Meteor Crater Observatory structure in the mid-1930s. Despite Hope's passing, Harry continued work on the building, and in the late 1930s finally opened the observatory to the public. A few years later, the Meteor Crater Observatory closed its doors due to lack of visitors and the large debt accrued during its construction. Then, in 1946, Dr. Harvey H. Nininger leased the building and on October 19 opened the doors once again. Inspired by a meteor he saw while teaching in Kansas in 1923, Dr. Nininger dedicated his life to the study of hurtling space debris and is known as the founder of the scientific study of meteorites.

The crater itself was located about 6 miles south of the observatory. Visitors climbed the dark and very narrow stairs of the tower and waited their turn at the telescope—all for only 25 cents! The museum also housed concessions, meteorite samples, and a detailed model showing the path Arizona's meteor took as it sailed through the earth's atmosphere, eventually crashing to the desert floor. A few years after its reopening the facility became officially known as the American Meteorite Museum. Visible for many miles, it must have been a remarkable site. Even today the ruins can be seen out in the distance on Interstate 40, beckoning to passing cars. The Meteorite Museum hosted its last stargazer in 1953. Dr. Nininger died in 1986.

CORNER IN AMERICAN METEORITE MUSEUM
OPPOSITE METEOR CRATER ON HIGHWAY 66 IN ARIZONA

TWO GUNS
c. 1948

Located halfway between Winslow and Flagstaff, no other town on Route 66 has such a frightening and storied past. In 1881, the story goes, more than 50 Navajo men, women, and children were slaughtered by a band of Apaches at a Navajo camp in the nearby Painted Desert. Navajo warriors tracked the Apaches, trapped them in a nearby cave, and quickly gathered sagebrush, wood, and anything else that would burn. The Navajos then built a fire at the entrance to the cave, which quickly filled with fire and smoke, then opened fire into the cave. They entered it the next day to find the charred and riddled remains of 42 Apaches. The cave is still known as the Apache Death Cave and carries with it a curse of bad luck to anyone who enters or disturbs the site. Other legends include rumors of loot left in a nearby canyon by train robbers .

By the 1950s, Two Guns had become a very popular stop along Route 66. What kid wouldn't want to see the Indian cliff dwellings, mountain lions, and the occasional cowboy or Indian? Stores, cafés, a service station, and a motel were also there for tired tourists. The concrete bridge through town crosses the Canyon Diablo and was listed on the National Register of Historic Places in 1988. The former roadside stop is now a crumbling ghost town. Stop and visit at your own risk.

WINONA TRADING POST, WINONA
c. 1955

In the early 1920s Billy Adams built a one-story rock structure from river stones and nearby Indian ruins and called it the Winona Trading Post. He offered necessities for modern motorists, including fan belts, coils, tools, and tires. Cold drinks and dry goods were also available. In 1924 a post office was established in the trading post, and Myrtle Adams became the first female postmaster in Arizona. Soon after completing the trading post, Billy Adams and his sons built 10 small wooden cabins, said to comprise one of the first motor courts in the United States. Each cabin measured 10x14 and featured a wood-burning stove, mirror, and washstand. In 1925, Adams built the two-story Winona Motel, once again of stone. The motel had 14 rooms upstairs and a small lobby below. Through the 1940s it was a beehive of activity, especially during World War II when convoys of troops would come through town. Billy's son Ralph recalls, "They would buy every bottle of pop and every candy bar we had and run us out completely in one visit."

The early 1950s saw a realignment of Route 66 to its current location, and a new trading post, including a cafe, tourist cabins, and service station, was built alongside the new alignment. Billy Adams and his family eventually left the post to become ranchers. The current owners bulldozed the motel, trading post, and campground.

WILLIAMS
c. 1940s

Founded in 1876, Williams was named for the famed mountaineer William Sherley Williams. The railroad officially arrived in town in 1882, and Williams quickly grew into a lumber and ranching center. In 1901, the Santa Fe Railway built a 60-mile spur to the Grand Canyon, and Williams has since been known as the "Gateway to the Grand Canyon." By the turn of the century, Williams, like many western railroad towns, had a rough-and-tumble reputation, its streets lined with brothels, saloons, opium dens, and gambling houses. One would be hard pressed to find any evidence of that reputation today. This quaint, small town has changed little since Route 66 carried the masses west and grape Nehi was the drink of the day. One can walk the streets, lined with many fine motels and cafés, and feel magically transported to a different time, when life's hectic pace was a crawl compared to today. All this thanks largely to the fact that Williams (nicknamed "Little Las Vegas" in late 1930s for its abundant neon signage) holds the honor of being the last bypassed town on Route 66; the final 6 miles of Interstate 40 bypassed the town on October 13, 1984. That same year, the Downtown Business District of Williams was placed on the National Register of Historic Places. The population, holding at about 3,000, has not changed much in 60 years—no doubt the residents like it that way.

BILL WILLIAMS AVENUE

Looking East

WILLIAMS ARIZONA

X703

Trasher's FOTOS

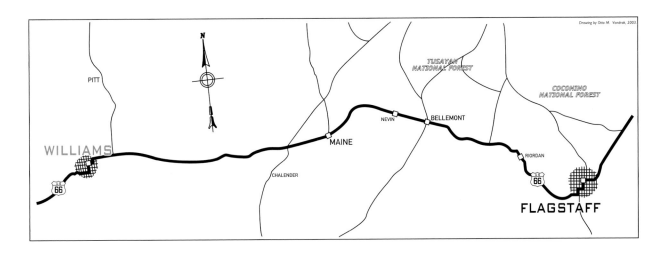

U. S. HIGHWAY 66, EASTBOUND THROUGH ASH FORK, ARIZONA

ASH FORK
c. 1948

In 1882 the Atlantic & Pacific Railway (later merged into the Santa Fe Railway) chose for a siding stop in the area now known as Ash Fork, named for the ash trees growing at the fork of nearby Ash Creek. The Ash Fork Livestock Company drove their cattle to the railhead, then shipped the animals east by rail. The cattle business—and the town—flourished. In 1893 Ash Fork was completely decimated by a fire, but was rebuilt and relocated to the other side of the tracks, where it still stands today.

A onetime hotbed of tourist activity, Ash Fork is today a shadow of its former self. The legendary Escalante, an elegant Harvey House hotel, was built along the Santa Fe tracks in 1907 and provided rail travelers fine dining and accommodations. In Route 66's heyday, dozens of motels, cafés, and gas stations lined the streets, offering much-needed services for travelers and vacationers. During World War II, regular troop trains brought thousands of servicepersons who eagerly spent their money there. When the Santa Fe moved its mainline 10 miles north of town in the 1950s, it marked the beginning of the end for the prosperous community. A fire destroyed many buildings in the early 1970s, and when the Interstate bypassed Ash Fork in 1979, the good times came to a screeching halt. Ash Fork, today known as the "Flagstone Capital of the U.S.A.," now sits quietly, waiting for the occasional stranded or hungry tourist.

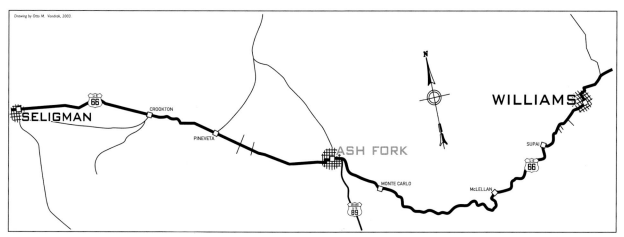

Drawing by Otto M. Vondrak, 2003.

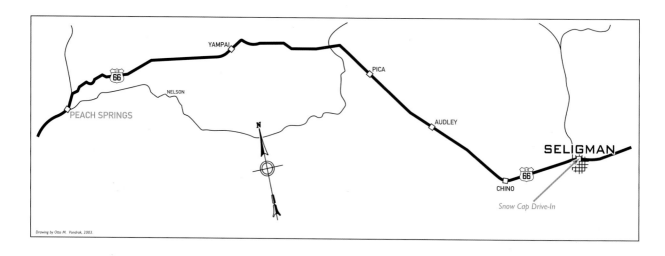

YAMPAI

66

NELSON

PEACH SPRINGS

PICA

AUDLEY

N

SELIGMAN

66

CHINO

Snow Cap Drive-In

Drawing by Otto M. Vondrak, 2003.

SNOW CAP DRIVE-IN, SELIGMAN
c. 1953

Juan Delgadillo, with help from his father, built the landmark Snow Cap in 1953. A Santa Fe employee at the time, Juan used materials discarded by the railroad, earning the nickname the "Santa Fe Pack Rat." Juan at first sought to become part of the Dairy Queen network, but was turned down, so he searched for other companies to affiliate with, eventually settling on the Snow Cap Corporation of Prescott, Arizona. Snow Cap folded, but Delgadillo kept the name.

"The Snow Cap has its own life, its own humor," says son Robert Delgadillo, who works at the restaurant alongside Juan, his brother John, and sister Cecilia. Upon entering the Snow Cap, be careful not to grab the fake door handle attached to the hinged side of the door. The menu offers "Dead Chicken" and "Cheeseburgers . . . with cheese." Ask for a napkin and Juan or Robert will offer a handful of used ones. But things were not always so lighthearted. Robert says his father was a "very serious person, serious about everything." So serious that 10 years after opening the Snow Cap doctors told him he was overstressed and needed to relax or he wasn't going to be around for long. He lightened up by making his customers laugh. As he became more comfortable in that role, the high jinks became a staple. Not to give away all of Delgadillo's material, but beware of the yellow mustard bottle.

PEACH SPRINGS
c. 1935

Peach Springs is located at the southern tip of the 1-million-acre Hualapai (pronounced *wall-a-pie*) Indian reservation and is home to their tribal headquarters. It was founded in the early 1880s when the Santa Fe Railway established a water station on the site and named it for the peach trees that grow at a nearby spring. It is said that Mormon missionaries planted the trees there while visiting the region in 1852. The onetime western terminus of the Santa Fe Railway located at Peach Springs included a roundhouse, Harvey House restaurant, and a stagecoach line that offered tours to the Grand Canyon beginning in the 1880s.

Prior to 1935, U.S. Highway 66 was a two-lane dirt road through the center of town flanked by a couple of service stations and auto courts. The old tourist courts are long gone, but in their place stands the newly constructed Hualapai Lodge run by the Hualapai tribe. Many improvements were made to the section of road from Seligman through Peach Springs to Hackberry. On the eastern approach to Peach Springs, several of the original sections of Route 66 are visible parallel to the newer version of Route 66. In 1978, Interstate 40 construction on the 70-mile section from Seligman to Kingman was completed, bypassing many small towns along the way including Peach Springs, which was bypassed by 36 miles, the most of any town along the route.

KINGMAN
c. 1948

Kingman, located on the gently sloping Hualapai Valley between the Hualapai and Cerbat mountain ranges, began as a railroad siding near Beale's Springs along the newly constructed Atlantic & Pacific Railway. Originally known as Middleton, the name was changed to Kingman in 1882 for Lewis Kingman, a line surveyor on the railroad. The first train pulled into town on March 28, 1883, and Kingman, the little camp by the tracks, has been a major transportation hub for the western states ever since. Kingman flourished during the early 1900s, and many of the buildings constructed then survive today, including the old Brunswick Hotel opened in 1909. Arizona's first commercial airport, Port Kingman, was also opened there in 1929.

Being such an important transportation gateway, it's ironic that most Kingman streets, including Route 66 through town, remained unpaved until around 1940. Stranger still is the fact that until 1941, Kingman was surrounded by fencing to keep wandering livestock off the streets. Kingman has a few Hollywood connections, as well. Clark Gable and Carole Lombard were married at St. John's Methodist church in 1939, and well-known Hollywood entertainer Andy Devine was raised in Kingman; Front Street (Route 66) was changed to Andy Devine Avenue in 1955. In 1953 Interstate 40 was completed in the area, making Kingman one of the first Mother Road cities to be bypassed.

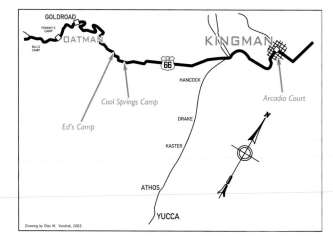

Drawing by Otto M. Vondrak, 2003.

ARCADIA COURT, KINGMAN
c. 1938

In its heyday the Arcadia Court catered to the "well to do." The back of this post card advertises, "Quiet and restful. Luxurious furnishings and the finest appointments for the fastidious guest. Healthiest climate (no humidity) and purest water. Special quarters for chauffeurs and maids." Eventually owners eliminated the garages to make way for more sleeping rooms, and during the early 1950s the Arcadia was remodeled and expanded to include 48 rooms. A heated swimming pool was also added later to keep up with the growing demands of the traveling public. After the Interstates bypassed their towns, many of the historic auto courts along Route 66 began a slow decline. The Arcadia Court was no exception. As motorists blew by

Kingman on I-40, the Arcadia Lodge, as it is now known, was left in the dust. Eventually, the classic auto court fell into a state of disrepair and local undesirables began calling the court home. Police were frequent visitors and the fine reputation the Arcadia Court once enjoyed became a distant memory. After a string of disinterested owners, the property was once again sold in 2001. Current managers Frank and Susan Brace are in the process of remodeling all the rooms. The drug dealers and prostitutes are long gone and with the help of the new owner, the Braces hope to once again make the Arcadia a stop of choice for the "fastidious guest."

COOL SPRINGS CAMP, WEST OF KINGMAN
c. 1939

N. R. Dunton built the Cool Springs Camp in the Black Mountains on the approach to Sitgreaves Pass in 1927. Being the resourceful person he was, he constructed the original buildings entirely out of stones gathered along the highway. In June 1936 Dunton sold the property to James and Mary Walker from Indiana. The Walker family, including their four children, moved to Cool Springs that summer and in January 1937 remodeled the business, adding a restaurant and bar. Mary divorced James after a few years and remarried a gentleman named Floyd Spidell, who added a full-service garage and guest cabins, turning the camp into a fully appointed travel stop. Eventually Mary and Floyd divorced and the business was left to Floyd.

The Cool Springs Camp was a very popular destination among travelers, as well as nearby Kingman residents. Well known for its fabulous chicken dinners, "locals" commuted as far as 20 miles to dine on the famous fowl. The Interstate bypassed this dangerous section of Highway 66 in the Black Mountains in 1952 in favor of a straighter and safer route to Topock, Arizona. After the realignment, business slowed to a crawl and the Cool Springs Camp was permanently shut down in 1964 when Floyd packed up and moved to Kingman. Ned Leuchtner of Kenilworth, Illinois, recently purchased the Cool Springs Camp site and at this writing was rebuilding the stone gas station.

COOLEST
SPOT
ON THE
DESERT

21 miles west
of Kingman,
9 miles east
of Oatman
ARIZONA
on U. S. Hwy. 66

E3910

ED'S CAMP, EAST OF GOLDROAD
c. 1947

Beginning the rugged approach to Sitgreaves Pass from the east, one of the most feared and dreaded sections on all of Route 66, travelers will notice the fading letters of Ed's Camp, spelled out in painted white rocks on the side of a hill. Lowell "Ed" Edgerton purchased the property that Ed's Camp sits on in the late 1930s, hoping to cash in on the ever-increasing flow of tourists. Throughout the 1930s and 1940s, Edgerton expanded his desert oasis to include a grocery store, gas station, trailer camp, and souvenir shop. It was a "camp" in every sense of the word—there were never any cabins or rooms at the site. Motorists on a budget would pull in and sleep in tents or in their cars. For $1, a tired traveler with a little bit of extra cash could sleep on a cot in a screened porch. Water was an-all-too precious commodity and was sold to guests on a per-bucket basis unless they paid the buck to spend the night—then it was free.

Edgerton went on to become a world-renowned figure in the field of geology. Amateur geologists came from around the world to hunt the area for precious stones, paying Edgerton a small fee for the privilege. In 1952, Route 66 was realigned around the Black Mountains from Kingman to Topock, bypassing the steep and treacherous mountain pass. Ed died in 1978, but his camp remains, for all intents and purposes undisturbed and hearkening back to better days.

OATMAN
c. 1929

Oatman, originally Vivian, sprang up from the blistering Mojave Desert when gold was discovered in 1902. After major gold strikes in 1908 and 1913, the population rose to as many as 10,000. By 1916 it was a bustling, thriving community. By the 1930s, gold strikes were few and mining operations began to diminish. As World War II wound up, the federal government ordered the remainder of the open mines closed, arguing the manpower was needed elsewhere. Thankfully, Route 66 ran directly through the center of town and the burgeoning tourist trade helped the community survive.

When 66 was rerouted in 1952, the Kingman *Daily Miner* reported, "One afternoon in 1952 traffic was coming steadily over Sitgreaves Pass, then it was silent. Someone rushed to Oatman with the news that they had cut the ribbon on the new section of U.S. Highway 66 between Kingman and Topock. Six of the seven service station families started to leave town the following day and owners of other businesses followed." After the bypass Oatman's population sank to a low of 60. The burros that worked in the mines were left behind. Their wild descendents wander Oatman's main street, looking for handouts and serving as one of the popular tourist attractions in Oatman. Another popular spot is the Oatman Hotel, where Clark Gable and Carole Lombard spent their honeymoon night. The room has been preserved and kept in its original state.

CALIFORNIA

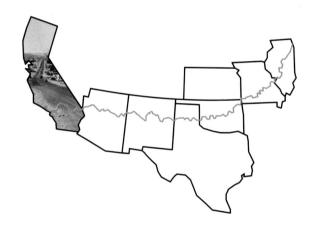

In the 1930s, countless Dust Bowl families left the drought-plagued heartland in search of a better life. The Great Depression was also in full swing and Route 66 to California was the escape route of choice. These early travelers who braved Sitgreaves Pass and perilous sections in Arizona must have first been disappointed in their destination. After crossing the Colorado River, expecting a glimpse of rich and fertile land filled with blossoming orange groves, they found more desert.

The first town after crossing the Colorado was Needles, where summer temperatures can soar to 125 degrees Fahrenheit. Imagine piling all your worldly possessions on an old Ford, tires barely keeping the rims from grinding on pavement, leaving all you knew behind, and suffering incredible heat and hardships, only to find more of what you just left behind. The Mojave Desert between Needles and Barstow, 150 blistering miles via the early alignment, was some of the most treacherous road on all of Route 66. Tiny hamlets along this stretch provided motorists with not much more than the essentials. Throughout Route 66's history, wrecker services along this section worked 24 hours a day, picking up stranded motorists or towing the really unlucky ones involved in accidents. During World War II the region was used by Patton to train his troops for battle against the Germans in North Africa.

Veterans of this blistering stretch of Route 66 knew to travel by night and to carry plenty of water. Once they reached Barstow, most Dust Bowl families left the Mother Road and headed north toward Bakersfield, hoping to find work in the farmlands of the San Joaquin Valley. Travel from Barstow to Los Angeles was relatively worry-free compared to the desert crossing, but not without its own perils. The Cajon Pass, "Gateway to Southern California," posed a formidable challenge as it wound its way down a difficult grade to San Bernardino. From there, 66 sliced through Upland, Azusa, Duarte, Arcadia, and Pasadena. The original western terminus of Route 66 was the intersection of Broadway and 7th Street in downtown Los Angeles. On January 1, 1936, the route was extended through Hollywood to Santa Monica, where it took a left-hand turn on to Lincoln Boulevard and ended at the intersection with Olympic Boulevard. Contrary to popular belief, Route 66 never reached the Santa Monica Pier or the Pacific Ocean.

Los Angeles saw so many alignment changes over the years that a complete guidebook, *Route 66 in Los Angeles County* by Scott R Piotrowski, was dedicated to unraveling its mysteries. One notable realignment, the Arroyo Seco Parkway, was considered the first freeway west of the Mississippi. Construction was completed on the Parkway in the late 1940s, and it is listed as a National Scenic Byway.

Whether you were a migrant family fleeing the Dust Bowl, an unemployed factory worker looking for a better life during the Great Depression, an actor dreaming of making it big in Hollywood, or simply taking the family on its annual summer vacation, reaching California was the collective dream and U.S. Highway 66 was the bright beacon that helped guide the masses and transform those dreams into reality.

NEEDLES
c. 1929

The town of Needles was established in 1883 as a burgeoning railroad town and mining hub. To this day the railroad is by far its largest employer. Known as "The Gateway to California," Needles got its name from the jagged, sharply pointed peaks of the Black Mountains southwest of the town. To say that it gets hot in this part of the country is a major understatement. Jack Rittenhouse, author of 1946's *A Guide Book to Highway 66:* "In the hot months, it is advisable to make the drive from Needles to Barstow, over the Mojave Desert, either in the evening, night or early morning hours. In any case, it is advisable to carry extra water for the car."

Needles is home to the ornate El Garces, a onetime Harvey House that served railroad customers until 1949. Today, the Friends of El Garces hope to restore the magnificent structure for future generations to enjoy. In 1973 Interstate 40 was completed and tourist traffic fell dramatically as cars disappeared. A few of the classic motels and cafés survive, but that's a relative term. In this part of the country, Route 66 was born out of crude dirt pathways and wooden-plank roads that twisted their way across the desert. The onetime concrete artery that fed life into the western part of our nation is slowly and begrudgingly returning to that desert, as America's Main Street begins its gradual decay and the Mojave slowly reclaims its own.

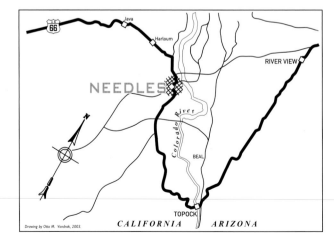

Drawing by Otto M. Vondrak, 2003.

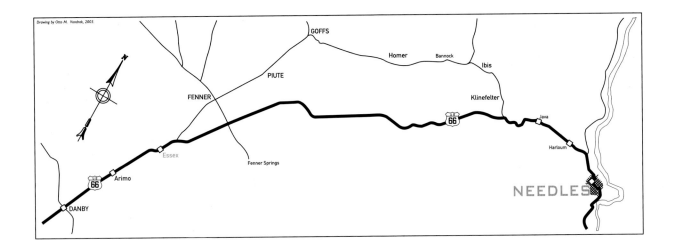

Drawing by Otto M. Vondrak, 2003.

ESSEX
c. 1942

It is rumored that the tiny Mojave Desert town of Essex was founded when an unlucky motorist broke down in the area. With no towing or service station for miles, he decided to stay and call this desert spot home. Being an enterprising sort, he opened a towing service with a café, and Essex was born, located on a section of road originally known as the National Old Trails Highway. In 1926 this road was redesignated U.S. Highway 66. During the late 1940s and the 1950s, Essex offered travelers and tourists all the essentials needed for desert travel, including towing services, gasoline, food, and water. Back in the days when tourist traffic regularly flowed through town, clean water was a precious commodity sold to

motorists at 10 cents per glass for drinking; unfiltered water was sold at 10 cents per gallon for car radiators. The Automobile Club of Southern California graciously installed a free drinking fountain in town, alleviating the outrageous charges levied by local businesses. This stone well-like structure still stands a couple of hundred feet from the onetime market and just a few feet south of the highway. Although no longer in service, it reminds us of the dangers that once confronted early motorists traveling the Mojave. The U.S. Postal Service is the only remaining Essex business still in operation. The café was reopened sometime in the 1990s but was eventually shut down and remains abandoned.

CADIZ SUMMIT SERVICE, CADIZ
c. 1946

Cadiz Summit Service was originally built in the 1920s by George and Minnie Tienken on the old alignment of U.S. Highway 66 that ran through Goffs and Fenner, California. In 1931, Route 66 was realigned from Goffs to create a straighter, more direct path. Undaunted, George and Minnie moved the business, buildings and all, to this new location about 18 miles west of Essex. After a long, hot, and often hazardous summer day's travel in the Mojave, this lonely California rest stop must have been a very welcome site. Standing in the now-deserted parking area, one can almost see and hear the hustle and bustle of hot and thirsty travelers looking for a cold drink or a quick snack.

Interstate 40 bypassed this section of Route 66 in 1972, cutting off its lifeblood and allowing another landmark roadside business to fall victim to the name of progress. Soon after the bypass, traffic along the route slowed to a trickle and Cadiz Summit closed its doors. In no time, vandals and looters took over and a fire finally destroyed what was left. Jack Rittenhouse, in his *Guide Book to Highway 66,* wrote of Cadiz Summit, "a handful of tourist cabins, a café and gas station comprise this desert oasis." No visible evidence of the cabins remains.

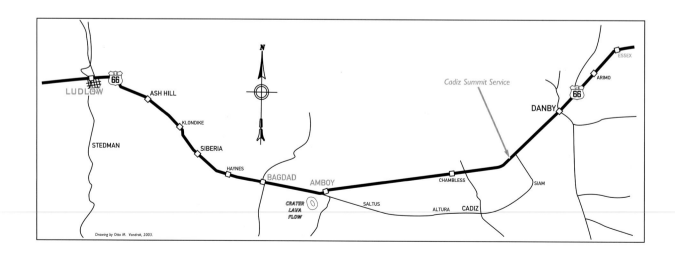

Drawing by Otto M. Vondrak, 2003.

AMBOY
c. 1946

Both Herman "Buster" Burris and Roy Crowl figure prominently in Amboy's growth during the glory days of Route 66. A native Texan, Burris was working as a mechanic at the nearby March Air Base when he met and married Crowl's daughter. He and Crowl went on to become business partners. In 1940 Burris opened a repair shop and in 1945 a café. A couple of cabins were also built to accommodate customers waiting for repairs. In 1948 he began construction on a motel that was completed in its present form in 1952. The famous "Roy's Motel" sign was built in 1959 and remains one of the most recognizable structures on all of Route 66.

"I used to think everybody in the world was driving through Amboy," said Burris. The town's population grew at a frantic pace as mechanics, waitresses, and motel help moved to the area. When Interstate 40 bypassed Amboy in the 1970s, "It was just like somebody put up a gate across Route 66. The traffic just plain stopped," recalled Burris. Through the years Burris expanded the business as opportunities arose, until one day he found he owned the whole town. In the early 1980s he put the complete town up for sale. The asking price: $350,000. Walt Wilson and Timothy White purchased Amboy in 2000 and rented the town out as a film location. In 2002 Amboy was once again put up for sale, this time on eBay, but the reserve price was not met and Amboy remains unsold.

BAGDAD
c. 1950s

The desert town of Bagdad began in 1883 as a small railroad stop. When the Orange Blossom and Lady Lou mines struck pay dirt around the turn of the century, the town of Bagdad became a major gold shipping point. As the mining industry declined, so did Bagdad's fortunes. In 1923 the town lost its post office and by 1937 the mines were closing at a rapid pace, but the Santa Fe depot remained to transport ore, and Bagdad continued to be a coal and water stop for steam engines.

By the 1940s most of the mines were closed and Bagdad, whose population once peaked at close to 600, dropped to about 20. Still, business from Route 66 traffic kept some of the town alive. Paul Limon, a onetime gas station attendant remembers, "Bagdad was a lively little place. People from all over the desert would come here because of the Bagdad Café, owned and operated by a woman named Alice Lawrence. The Bagdad Café was the only place for miles around with a dance floor and jukebox." The café, gas station, cabins, and market continued to serve travelers until 1972, when the Interstate opened to the north. The 1988 film *Bagdad Café,* inspired by the town and its café, was actually filmed in Newberry Springs, 50 miles west of Bagdad. In 1991 the site was used as storage for a natural gas project and the town was wiped clean. Today, there is no evidence the town ever existed.

LUDLOW
c. 1940

"In comparison with neighboring towns, Ludlow is a metropolis," read the 1939 WPA guide to U.S. Highway 66 in California. The population of Ludlow, including railroad crews' families and miners who worked the nearby Bagdad Chase Mines, reached a peak of about 150. Established in 1882, the town was named for William B. Ludlow, who repaired railcars for the nearby Santa Fe Railway. This area of the Mojave was so isolated that the Santa Fe had to import water in tanker cars. The water was then pumped into an elevated storage tank and gravity fed to Ludlow's thirsty residents until 1965 when Ludlow's first well was dug. The Murphy Brothers Mercantile Store was the most prominent business, along with a "mall" consisting of a pool hall/tavern, grocery store, and restaurant that served locals and travelers alike. When Route 66 was the main artery to the West, Ludlow enjoyed a booming travel business. That ended when Interstate 40 bypassed the town in 1972, marking Ludlow's second economic collapse, the first being the decline of mining in the 1940s. Today, Ludlow consists of a couple of service stations, a café, and a motel to serve the needs of Interstate travelers and Route 66 explorers.

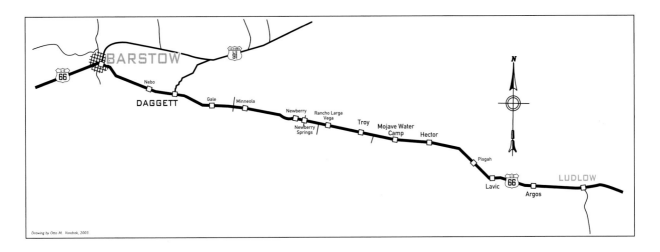

BARSTOW
c. 1948

More than 150 miles of harsh, sun-baked terrain awaited motorists departing Needles for Barstow. Previously known as Waterman, the town's name was changed in 1886 to honor Santa Fe President William Barstow Strong after that railroad built a depot in town. (His middle name was used because Kansas already had a "Strong" station on the line.) A new railroad depot, Casa del Desierto, completed in 1911, was added to the National Register of Historic Places in 1975. Today, the beautifully restored "House in the Desert" is home to the Route 66 Mother Road Museum (www.Barstow66museum.itgo.com).

During Barstow's early years the town was located on the north side of the railroad tracks but as a result of frequent expansion of the railroad, was eventually relocated to the south. Four-lane Interstate 15 was completed from Barstow to Victorville in 1958, shortening the distance between the two towns by 5 miles. The bypass, as elsewhere, had a tremendous negative impact on Barstow's downtown business district, but the city found new life at its eastern edge. There, the intersection of Interstate 40 and Interstate 15 functions as an ideal refueling point and rest stop.

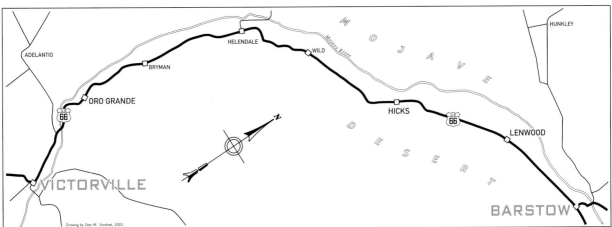

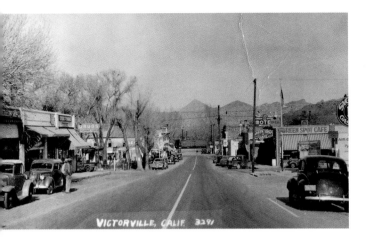 

VICTORVILLE
c. 1939

The small town of Victorville is located 97 miles northeast of Los Angeles at the western edge of the Mojave Desert. In 1885, the Southern California Railroad built a station there and the area became known as Huntington Station. It was later dubbed "Victor" after the railroad's construction superintendent, Jacob Nash Victor, then renamed Victorville when the mail service began confusing Victor, California, with Victor, Colorado. Victorville, a favorite location for filming western "B movies" in the 1960s, has survived and grown since the Interstate totally bypassed the town in 1972, as is evidenced by the population increase from 11,200 in 1972 to 71,224 today. At the time the above postcard photograph was taken, the city's population was listed as approximately 2,500.

Route 66 ran west through Victorville on D Street, making a right turn onto 7th Street, and continuing through town toward the steep grade of the Cajon Pass on its way to San Bernardino before terminating in Los Angeles. The popular California Route 66 Museum (www.califrt66museum.org) is located on Route 66 in "Old Town" Victorville and is housed in the onetime Red Rooster Café building, where the *Jazz Singer,* starring Neil Diamond, was filmed.

ROUTE 66
LOST & FOUND
RUINS AND RELICS REVISITED, VOLUME 2

RUSSELL A. OLSEN

Voyageur Press

PREFACE & ACKNOWLEDGMENTS

The allure of Route 66 can put a powerful spell on a person. I offer myself as a prime example. It will sneak up and pounce on you without warning. One day you appear normal and seem fine, then, before you realize it, you find yourself strapped in your automobile traveling thousands of miles to search for and photograph Route 66 icons. I have never been able to pinpoint or put into words the reason for this addiction to the road, but its hold on me is formidable. The thrill of finding an old café or motel or, better yet, a long, abandoned portion of highway is exhilarating. Anyone who enjoys exploring our country's old roads or even its old pioneer trails, like the Santa Fe and Oregon trails, knows what I am talking about.

Something about these historic pathways draws you in, and the more you dig, the deeper you want to go. So much history of these early roads and trails was never recorded or has been lost forever. Photographic documentation of the pioneer trails is mostly nonexistent. What a treat it would be to open the pages of a book and see the way the trail appeared when wagons blazed dusty tracks and pioneers and traders tackled the formidable Santa Fe. What did the Iron Springs Stage Station or the crossing at Turkey Creek look like during the heyday of the Santa Fe Trail? I have spent hours daydreaming and imagining these scenes.

In a hundred years will we look at Highway 66 as we do the old pioneer trails? Will Route 66 be viewed as an ancient and primitive trail once used by pioneering tourists? Will roads be unnecessary by then? Will there be anything left to explore? Will someone a hundred years in the future wonder what travel was like on Old Route 66, just as many of us today wonder about the dusty old wagon trails? These are the questions I hope to answer in the *Route 66 Lost & Found* books.

In its present state, Route 66 is a 2,400-mile museum of early auto travel, but sadly we lose a bit of that history in the name of "progress" every day. My goal is to document as much of this historic highway and its roadside culture as possible with the hope that future generations will look on these books as I do books on the old western trails. Can you imagine someone in the distant future being shocked by the fact that you actually had to stop for gasoline, or amazed that people actually used machines that needed such a primitive fuel to operate? I am sure that if you stop and think about the covered wagons of 150 years ago, your thoughts would be similar to those of someone 150 years from now regarding Route 66 and automobile travel. When you open this book and thumb through its pages, it is my sincere hope that you feel and experience a portion of the spell that Route 66 has put on me.

There are many people to thank for helping me with this book. I owe a great deal of gratitude to the people who allowed me access to their private postcard collections: Laurel Kane, Jerry McClanahan, Jeff Meyer, Steven Rider, Jim Ross, Joe Sonderman, and Mike Ward.

The following people I thank for helping with research and supplying vintage photos of many of the subjects appearing in this book: Nick Adam, Kathy Anderson, Tim Burchett, Marion Clark, C. H. "Skip" Curtis, Linda Drake, Mike Dragovich, Janice Lauritzen, John Hockaday, Richard Mangum, Scott Piotrowski, Bill Thomas, John Weiss, Betty Wheatley, and the late Tom Teague. Special thanks go out to Russell Adams at Schulman Photo Lab in Hollywood and to Chris More and Zach Allred for allowing me access to the PG&E facility for the Red Rock Bridge Photo. Thanks, also, to Brett Bather for technical assistance.

Finally, a very special thank you to Mardjie and Vince Paradero of Frank's Custom Lab in North Hollywood for their invaluable assistance in the making of this book.

ILLINOIS

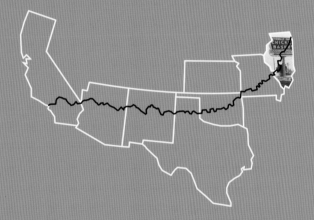

DELL RHEA'S CHICKEN BASKET, WILLOWBROOK
c. 1946

Adjacent to the current location of Dell Rhea's Chicken Basket, a man named Irv Kolarik owned and operated a service station where he not only serviced automobiles but also served up pie, coffee, and cold sandwiches at a small lunch counter. Unhappy with the dirty environment of the gas station, Kolarik thought selling more food would be more to his liking. One day, two local women overheard his complaining and offered to teach him how to cook fried chicken using their tasty recipe if he would agree to buy his chickens from them. A deal was struck and the rest, as they say, is history.

The chicken dishes became so popular that he quickly outgrew his small lunch counter and expanded by converting his two service bays into dining rooms. Eventually a new building was needed; in June 1946 the business moved to its current location and became known as the "Nationally Famous Chicken Basket." Prior to 1946 the business was known both as Club Roundup and the Triangle Inn. In one of his more elaborate schemes developed to attract customers to a roadside business, Kolarik had the restaurant's parapet roof flooded with water and hired professional ice skaters to skate on the rooftop during the winter months. Spotlights aimed at the skaters created quite a scene at night. People would come from miles around to view the rooftop spectacle and get a bite to eat, just as Kolarik had hoped.

The property changed ownership two times during the late 1950s and early 1960s. When four-lane Route 66 bypassed the Chicken Basket, the restaurant fell on hard times and was eventually repossessed. In 1963 Dell Rhea and his wife, Grace, bought the business from the bank and changed the name to Dell Rhea's Chicken Basket. Today the restaurant looks much as it did when it opened in 1946. The only alteration is an enclosed outdoor patio, which serves as another dining room. In June 1992 Dell Rhea's Chicken Basket was inducted into the Illinois Route 66 Hall of Fame. Rhea's son, Patrick, purchased the restaurant from his family in 1986 and is responsible for many of the tasty dishes, including the secret chicken marinade, served up at the Chicken Basket today. Patrick is quite proud of the fact that all his dishes are prepared using the finest fresh ingredients and is quick to point out that his chicken is marinated for a full 24 hours before being hand-breaded. Anyone hungry?

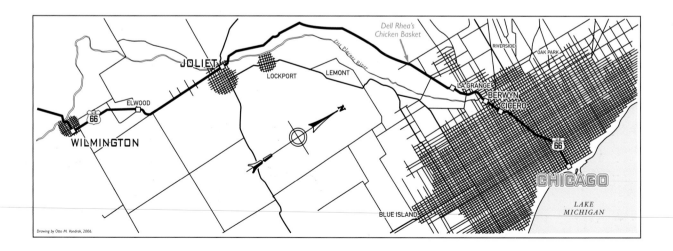

Drawing by Otto M. Vondrak, 2006.

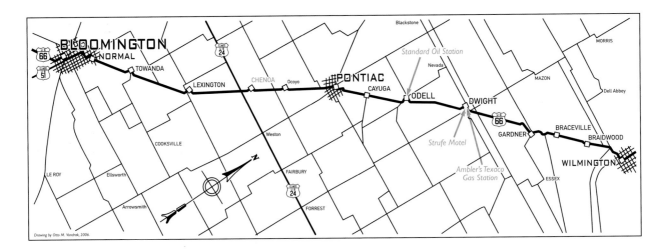

Drawing by Otto M. Vondrak, 2006.

AMBLER'S TEXACO GAS STATION, DWIGHT
c. 1933

Jack Schore built the original structure at the corner of Route 66 and Illinois Route 17 with the help of his son Paul in 1933. The station holds the honor of being one of the longest-operating service stations on all of Route 66. It uses a design commonly called the "domestic style" gas station that was developed by the Standard Oil Company in 1916. This neighborhood-friendly design stemmed from growing community opposition to the often-unsightly gas stations growing more common in and around towns during that time. It was an obvious effort to create gas stations that would blend in with their surrounding neighborhoods. This design also created a secure, homelike atmosphere that oil executives hoped would attract out-of-town travelers.

In 1936 Vernon VonQualon leased the property from Schore and operated the station for two years before turning it over to Basil "Tubby" Ambler, who operated the station from 1938 until 1965.

During the early 1940s Ambler added a service bay, allowing the business to offer service and repairs year-round. In 1965, Ambler sold the station to Earl Kochler, who in turn sold it to Royce McBeath. It changed hands one more time when McBeath sold it to Phil Becker on March 4, 1970. Becker had begun working there in 1964, just one year before Ambler sold to Kochler. One year after Becker purchased the station, Texaco abruptly stopped supplying the station its gasoline. Becker signed on with Marathon, and the station was known as Becker's Marathon Gas Station for over 26 years.

The station was listed on the National Register of Historic Places on November 29, 2001. Although it changed hands many times, Ambler's significant 27-year ownership prompted the station to be listed as Ambler's Texaco Gas Station. It's currently being restored to its 1940 appearance and will be utilized as a Route 66 interpretive center.

STRUFE MOTEL, DWIGHT
c. 1952

The Strufe Motel was built on the southwest end of Dwight, just south of the Ambler station. It began life as a gas station, built and owned by Martin and Mehta Paulsen, who had emigrated from Denmark. Sometime after the station was completed, the Paulsens built six tourist cabins out back and joined them together with a single roof, creating a carport for each cabin. During the time that Martin and Mehta owned the business, it was called Paulsen's Court.

John and Dorothy Strufe purchased the business in 1952 and renamed the complex the Strufe Motel. For the first couple of years, the Strufes worked and lived in the station with their son, Frederick, who was four years old when they purchased it. In 1959 they decided to discontinue the sale of gasoline. The pumps were removed, and the station was converted into a living space and an office for the

motel. Eventually the carports were enclosed, creating four additional rooms and a large utility room. Brick veneer was used to cover the front and sides, giving the individual units the appearance of a single ten-unit building. Following the remodeling the name was changed to the Arrow Motel.

After the tragic death of the Strufes in an automobile accident in 1968, Frederick continued to operate the motel until 1973, when it was sold to Norris and Betty Ruff. The motel changed hands again in 1977 and 1989 when the William DuPont and James Moyemont families entered into a partnership. Michael Moyemont eventually bought out all the partners and is now sole owner of the property. The ten-unit motel has been converted into two apartments and sits quietly concealed behind new vinyl siding, which covers the old brick veneer.

STANDARD OIL STATION, ODELL
c. 1932

Built in 1932 by Patrick O'Donnell, this gas station sits on the southwest side of Odell in Livingston County, just a few yards from the fabled Mother Road. Like many of the gas stations in this part of the country, it was built using original plans developed by Standard Oil of Ohio in 1916. The basic design of the "domestic style" gas station, as it was dubbed, consisted of a simple houselike structure with an attached canopy. The Odell station featured Standard Oil products for many of its early years, but by 1940 it was distributing Phillips 66 through its pumps. Prior to 1952 the station discontinued selling Phillips 66 and switched allegiance to Sinclair. The last drop of gas sold at the station was Sinclair brand in 1967.

During the glory days of Route 66, competition among gas station owners was fierce. There were more than ten stations on the short stretch of Route 66 in and around Odell. To attract more business, O'Donnell added service bays in 1937. When the bypass appeared and other stations fell by the wayside from lack of business, the service bay proved to be the station's saving grace.

In 1952 Robert Close leased the station from O'Donnell and bought the property after O'Donnell's passing in 1967. Close and his family lived in a converted café adjacent to the filling station until the café burned down sometime in the 1970s. Close eventually began doing bodywork at the station and continued until the Village of Odell bought the property in 1999.

Efforts to have the historic Standard Oil Station listed on the National Register of Historic Places began in 1995 and were rewarded with the station's listing in November 1997. Preservation efforts began in earnest in 1998, when volunteers from the Route 66 Association of Illinois began working diligently to preserve this Route 66 icon for future generations. The beautifully restored filling station is currently operated as a museum and information center.

CHENOA
c. 1927

Chenoa had its humble beginnings in 1854, when Mathew T. Scott acquired thousands of acres of prairie wilderness in the area. He proceeded to lay out lots and streets for the yet-unnamed town. It was prime property, located at the intersection of the Toledo, Peoria & Western and the Chicago & Alton railroads. The town's first building was the Farmers Store, built in 1855 by J. B. Lenney, who is often referred to as the Father of Chenoa. By the time the town was founded as Chenoa, a native word meaning "white dove," the thousands of Indians who at one time made the region their home had long since been removed by the U.S. government to areas west of the Mississippi River.

Chenoa has seen several routings of Highway 66 over the years, including a four-lane version with a railroad crossing that caused long traffic jams as travelers in both directions waited anxiously to proceed. Chenoa has long catered to Route 66 travelers. During the highway's heyday, gas stations, motels, and cafés (including the famous Steve's Café that can be seen in the vintage photo) lined the town's streets. (For more information on Steve's Café, see the first *Route 66 Lost & Found*.)

Land for a tourist park, at first simply called "Tourist Park" (presently known as Red Bird Park), was donated by Scott. The park is a testament to Chenoa's early desire to attract and serve automobile travelers. Tourists were allowed to camp free of charge in the park until the land was leased and a tourist court was built on the property. Many original, vintage buildings remain there, including a structure that has continuously housed a pharmacy (now Chenoa Pharmacy) since 1889.

Like many of the small communities located along this stretch of Route 66, the citizens of Chenoa are proud of their Route 66 heritage and truly make you feel welcome in their community.

PALMS GRILL CAFÉ, ATLANTA
c. 1934

James Robert Adams opened the Palms Grill Café in August 1934, boasting "home cooking, quick service and courteous treatment." Adams was born just outside of Atlanta but moved to Los Angeles after serving in World War I. He shuttled back and forth between Los Angeles and Atlanta but spent a majority of his time in California. He named the café in reference to his time spent in that state. In fact, the interior was decorated as homage to a restaurant Adams frequented near his home in Los Angeles.

The café occupied the north half of a building known as the Downey Building, which was built after the Civil War in 1867. With five tables and two counters, the seating capacity for the café was about 30.

From the beginning the "The Grill," as it was locally known, was more than just a source of good food. Soon after its opening, the café developed into an integral part of Atlanta's social scene. Many Atlanta teenagers got their first taste of employment waiting tables or grilling short orders there. Behind the kitchen at the rear of the building was a dance hall, where locals would gather on Wednesday nights to cut loose and socialize. The dance hall was also used to host large private gatherings and parties.

In January 1940 the Palms Grill Café became a designated Greyhound Bus stop. A small light at the bottom of the neon sign out front signaled bus drivers when passengers were waiting to board. From the late 1940s through the 1950s, the café became *the* place for Atlanta High School students to meet and eat. In the late 1960s, however, after Highway 66 traffic was routed away from the center of town, the Palms Grill Café served up its final dinner. The last owner of the Downey Building, John Hawkins, remodeled the interior into a living and work space. Upon his passing in 2002, the Hawkins family donated the building to the Atlanta Public Library and Museum. The vintage interior of the Palms Grill Café is currently being restored. The original Downey Building was listed on the National Register of Historic Places in 2004.

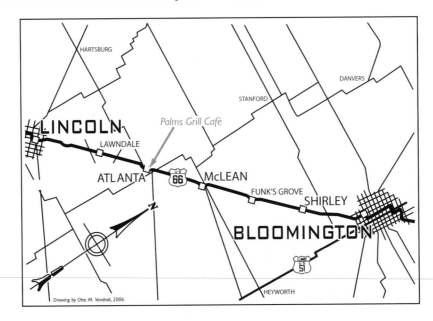

Drawing by Otto M. Vondrak, 2006.

ART'S MOTEL AND RESTAURANT, FARMERSVILLE
c. 1955

In 1932 Art McAnarney and Marty Gorman became business partners, operating everything from speakeasies and gas stations to dance halls and casinos in and around Farmersville. In 1937 McAnarney decided to go it alone and sold his share of the business back to Gorman. McAnarney leased a building that once housed the two-story Hendricks Brothers' Café and Gas Station and went into business for himself. He continued operating a restaurant and gas station, as well as renting six cabins for overnight guests, until the building caught fire in 1952, destroying the second floor. The main-floor dining room was salvageable; McAnarney rebuilt the business, utilizing the old dining room and the foundation, but opted for a single-story structure.

McAnarney died in 1957, leaving the business to his sons, Elmer and Joe. By that time, two-lane Route 66 in Illinois was almost nonexistent, having given way to the new and updated four-lane version. In 1960 the sons added a 13-room L-shaped motel that still stands today. When Interstate 55 was completed in the mid-1970s, it ran right in front of the property. An exit for Farmersville was built, and, as luck would have it, Art's was conveniently located near the on/off ramp, averting what would otherwise have spelled the end of the business. Although Art's Motel and Restaurant continued to operate, as of this writing it's closed and looking for a new owner. In 1995 Art's was inducted in to the Illinois Route 66 Hall of Fame.

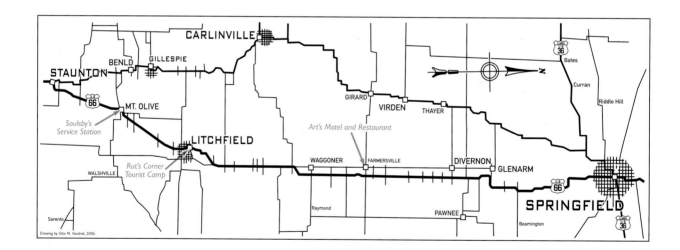

Drawing by Otto M. Vondrak, 2006.

RUT'S CORNER TOURIST CAMP, LITCHFIELD
c. 1929

Russell "Ruts" Brawley built Rut's Corner Tourist Camp just a few years after it was decided that Highway 66 would run through the town of Litchfield. A single row of gable-roofed cabins sat on one side of Brawley's property. A structure containing five guest units was positioned perpendicular to the cabins; for customers' convenience, each unit had a covered garage with a private entry. A community bathhouse was provided for guests of both the cabins and of the rooms.

A café was eventually added but burned to the ground in 1936. Olind McPherson, a one-time employee, remembers, "The fire was so hot that coins were melted together." The café was quickly rebuilt bigger and better, with room to serve upwards of 150 hungry guests. T-bone steak dinners were 40 cents.

"Rut's Corner was one of the busiest and most popular spots between Chicago and St. Louis," says McPherson. "The slot machines were the big thing." Brawley would say to him, "When a crowd gathers around the slot machines don't worry about cleaning up or anything. Just make sure the customers have change to feed the machines." McPherson also remembers galvanized wash basins of change so heavy that two men had to lift them. "That's how popular the slot machines were," he says.

A filling station was added later, making Rut's Corner a full-service tourist stop. Rut's closed sometime in the late 1950s. McPherson began cutting hair and has owned a barbershop for over 60 years. He remains in Litchfield and, at age 82, continues to cut hair. "I still work three days a week giving haircuts but now it's by appointment only," he says proudly.

RUT'S CORNER CAFE, ROUTE U. S. 66, LITCHFIELD, ILL.

SOULSBY'S SERVICE STATION, MOUNT OLIVE
c. 1926

Henry Soulsby was a southern Illinois coal miner by trade, following in his father's footsteps. Injury forced Soulsby to retire from mining sometime in the mid-1920s. In 1926, betting that the new U.S. Highway 66 would pass through Mount Olive, he used his life savings to purchase property on which he planned to build a gas station. With help from his young son, Russell, he proceeded to build a small, 30x12 structure of his own design. After high school, Russell joined his father in the business full time, while his sisters, Ola and Wilma, pitched in on a part-time basis. When Henry retired, Russell and Ola took over the daily operation of the station.

In 1937 the station was doubled in size but was never large enough for a repair bay. All repairs were performed outdoors on a ramp situated on the south side of the building. Following a stint in the military as a communications technician during World War II, Russell Soulsby returned to the station and quickly began utilizing his experience to repair radios and, later, televisions. After the interstate bypass was built in the late 1950s and automobile traffic dwindled, his television-repair business proved to be his mainstay. In 1991 Soulsby's discontinued the sale of gasoline but kept the station store open to sell soda, add the occasional quart of oil, and greet the growing number of tourists traveling the old road. In 1993 Soulsby closed his doors for good and sold the property in 1997 to Mike Dragovich in a public auction. Soulsby passed away in 1999. As a tribute, his funeral procession passed under the station's canopy on the way to the cemetery.

In 2003 Dragovich led volunteers in a major restoration effort that gave the station back its post–World War II color scheme. Today, looking like something out of a time machine, Soulsby's stands as a fitting tribute to Russell Soulsby and the glory days of Route 66.

LUNA CAFÉ, MITCHELL
c. 1931

Irma Rafalala is given credit for building the two-story Luna Café in 1924, two years prior to the designation of Highway 66. The foundation was dug using old-fashioned mule power and a large scoop, recalls 82-year-old Mitchell resident Bud Eberhart. The restaurant/bar was located on the main floor, while bedrooms, often used by railroad workers, were located upstairs.

One of the oldest continuously run establishments on the Mother Road, the Luna Café has a colorful history that revolves around gangsters, upstairs brothels, and basement gambling. As co-owner Alan Young says, "It's hard to separate fact from fiction." One of the many rumors surrounding the Luna is that Al Capone and his gang regularly stopped at the café when traveling between St. Louis and Chicago. High-stakes gambling reportedly took place in the basement on a regular basis and probably was one of the reasons for Capone's alleged visits.

Another unconfirmed story is that the upstairs bedrooms were often used for prostitution. As the legend goes, when the neon cherry was lit on the vintage sign out front, the ladies were waiting and available upstairs. According to a current tenant who resides upstairs, "There was a bell in each room. They would ring from downstairs to let the girls know who was wanted." The wiring for the bells is rumored to still be there.

In its early days the Luna Café catered to an upscale crowd, and much of its well-to-do clientele came from nearby St. Louis. The 1931 photo shows a painted sign on the side of the building advertising Budweiser and the restaurant fare. Young assured me that the sign still exists, albeit hidden under the newer siding.

Today the Luna Café is a neighborhood tavern catering mostly to locals. However, when tourist travel on Historic Route 66 is at its peak during the summer months, people from all over the world can be seen sitting at tables eating sandwiches and at the bar drinking cold brews. The Luna Café's roadhouse charm oozes from every corner, and the myriad stories, whether fact or fiction, only add to it. It does not take much of an imagination to visualize Capone and his gang sitting at a back table, making plans for a future heist or counting the take from the gambling downstairs.

The Luna Café was inducted into the Illinois Route 66 Hall of Fame in June 2004 and is currently owned by Alan Young and Larry Wofford. It is a great spot to wet your whistle.

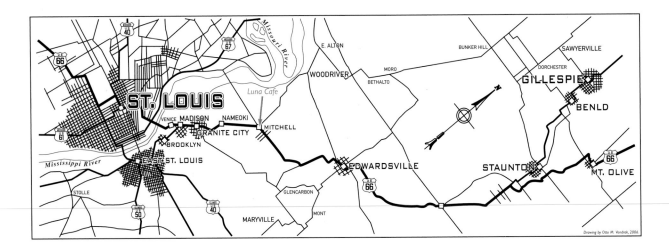

Drawing by Otto M. Vondrak, 2006

MISSOURI

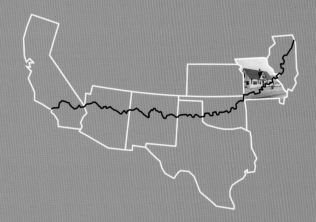

CORAL COURT, MARLBOROUGH
c. 1942

John Carr built the fabled Coral Court just outside the city limits of St. Louis. The motel was painstakingly designed by architect Adolph L. Struebig, and construction began in summer 1941. By early 1942 the Coral Court greeted its first guest. Ten single-story units, with two rooms and two garages per unit, and an office structure were included. Almost immediately the Coral Court became a standout. The Streamline Moderne style, the elegant veneer of ceramic-glazed brick, and artful glass-block windows made it one-of-a-kind.

In 1946, 23 additional units designed by architect Harold T. Tyre were built using the same materials and varying only slightly from the original ten units. The new units featured triangular glass-block windows, but the overall look of the Coral Court remained. Another expansion took place in 1953 with the addition of three more ordinary-looking two-story units, also designed by Tyre, at the rear of the property. A swimming pool was added in the early 1960s.

Carr died in 1984, leaving the Coral Court to his wife, Jessie, and head housekeeper, Martha Shutt. Jessie and her second husband, Robert Williams, operated the business until August 20, 1993. Over time a lack of maintenance took its toll. During its later years the Coral Court began a swift decline, even garnering quite a racy reputation. The fact that you could park in a garage, close the garage door, and enter the unit from inside the garage made the Coral Court a perfect rendezvous for star-crossed lovers. No guest vehicles were visible to jealous spouses driving through the grounds. As if that weren't enough, rooms could be rented in three-hour blocks.

Beginning in 1987 preservation groups fought to save the Coral Court from an untimely demise. The Coral Court was listed on the National Register of Historic Places on April 25, 1989. Sadly, the motel, except for one unit, was demolished in June 1995, and the new owners, Conrad Properties, began construction of the Oak Knoll Manor on the old Coral Court grounds.

Jessie (Carr) Williams passed away on October 15, 1996, a year after the razing of the Coral Court (Robert Williams had died on May 18, 1994).

The Coral Court's history is full of wonderful stories and anecdotes, which are covered in detail in *Tales from the Coral Court* by Shellee Graham. Luckily for fans of the Coral Court, the Missouri Museum of Transportation, with help from many volunteers, worked for weeks to disassemble a complete Coral Court building prior to the rest of the motel's demolition. The building was stored at the museum and rebuilt in all its glory, so that future generations will be able to view this work of art that just also happened to be a motel.

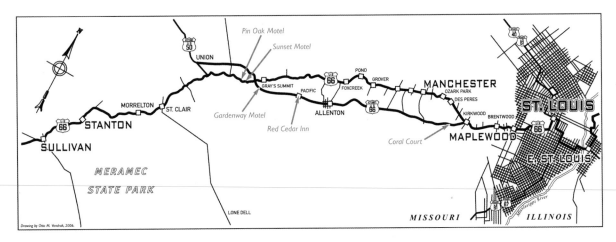

Drawing by Otto M. Vondrak, 2006.

RED CEDAR INN, PACIFIC
c. 1941

Brothers Bill and James Smith built the Red Cedar Inn in 1934 out of red cedar logs, which were cut from the family farm in nearby Villa Ridge and hauled to the construction site on a Ford Model AA truck. The structure's logs were all hewn with an ax, while the foundation was dug using mule power.

Soon after the inn's opening, sometime in 1935, a barroom was added to the facility. During the early years the inn offered gasoline service from two pumps out front. The sale of gasoline was eventually halted, and all efforts were focused on the restaurant business. In 1935, acting as manager of operations, James Smith II hired 19-year-old Katherine Brinkman to wait tables. It was the hiring of his life—the two soon fell in love and were married in 1940. Katherine and James II eventually purchased the business from his father in 1944.

Alongside son James III and daughter Ginger, the couple ran the business until James II retired in 1972. In 1987 Ginger and her father reopened the Red Cedar Inn with a little help from Katherine, who continued to bake the restaurant's delicious brownies.

The Red Cedar Inn was a classic example of the family-run businesses that proliferated on the highway during the glory days of Route 66. These businesses were slapped together with guts and hard work. Some continue to operate today, requiring even harder work to survive. Like the Red Cedar Inn, many have been handed down from generation to generation. Officially listed on the National Register of Historic Places on June 22, 2003, the Red Cedar Inn unfortunately ceased operation in 2005 and was up for sale at the time of this book's publication.

GARDENWAY MOTEL, GRAY SUMMIT
c. 1950

On the 30-mile stretch of Highway 66 between St. Louis and the Missouri Botanical Garden Arboretum at Gray Summit, the roadside was once lined with thousands of decorative shrubs, lush trees, and native flowers. The National Park Service and the Missouri State Highway Commission, in conjunction with the Missouri Botanical Garden, combined forces to create this remarkable landscaping and preserve the natural indigenous plant life of Missouri for future generations. Billed as the Henry Shaw Gardenway, in honor of the man who founded the Missouri Botanical Garden back in 1858, the project was completed in 1937.

In 1945 Louis B. Eckelkamp built his Colonial-style motel at the western edge of the Gardenway, near his home and adjacent to the Missouri Botanical Garden Arboretum. By 1954 the Gardenway Motel featured "Twenty-five Modern Cabins with Tile Baths." The motel eventually grew to also include 41 guest rooms.

The beautiful Streamline Moderne Gardenway sign beckoning motorists near the edge of the road sits in stark contrast to the motel's sprawling American Colonial architecture. When lit up, this sign stands out as the ultimate in classic Route 66 motel signage. Today the motel still waits patiently to serve vacationers and business travelers. The neon sign, on the other hand, waits to be brought back to life, longing for the flick of the switch that will once again breathe life into its colorful neon glass.

SUNSET MOTEL, VILLA RIDGE
c. 1942

Built in the early 1940s, the 12-unit Sunset Motel stands out as one of the more distinctive motels of the era. Located 38 miles west of St. Louis, the Sunset was built of beige brick and laid out in a V shape in which the exterior center of the V served as a community area equipped with ice and soda machines. One of the more unusual aspects of this motel is the fact that it was built with two entrances per unit: one entrance in front of each unit overlooking a sprawling, beautifully landscaped lawn area, and the other providing entrance from the parking lot and driveway behind the structure.

Today the motel stands much as it did when it was built over 60 years ago. The original eye-catching signage also remains intact and over the years has evolved into a Route 66 must-see photo op. "Twelve Units, Twelve Baths, Panel Ray Heat, Beautyrest Mattresses and Quiet" was the advertising copy that attracted weary motorists to the Sunset. The interstate bypass in 1967 added an exclamation point to the word "Quiet," and the Sunset Motel now sits empty and silent, fading in the golden twilight.

PIN OAK MOTEL - RT. 1, VILLA RIDGE, MO.

PIN OAK MOTEL, VILLA RIDGE
c. 1953

The Pin Oak Motel was built around 1940 some 40 miles west of St. Louis and was named for the beautiful pin oak trees that dominate the local landscape. The Pin Oak was originally laid out with two sets of two buildings. The buildings were joined by common carports and faced each other across a courtyard. Originally just eight units were available, but by the early 1950s more units had been added and the carports were enclosed. Eventually the room count grew to 28.

A member of the American Motor Hotel Association, the Pin Oak was billed as "a better court for better people" and was advertised as having "clean, ultra-modern units." In the early 1960s, free air conditioning, free TV, and new carpets were added to the list of amenities. In 1967, however, Interstate 44 bypassed the area and, like so many other motels, the Pin Oak fell on hard times. Eventually converted into a self-storage facility, the old Pin Oak Motel stands as a relic to the glory days of Route 66, safely storing memories of its past alongside family treasures within its aging walls.

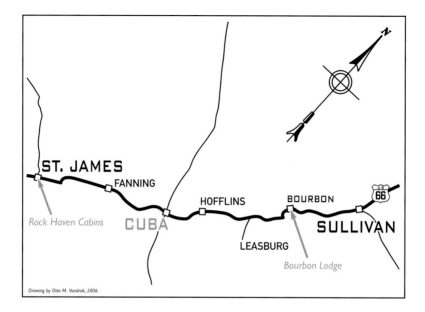

Drawing by Otto M. Vondrak, 2006.

BOURBON LODGE, BOURBON
c. 1940

Sometime during the 1850s, a store owner by the name of Richard Turner began selling a popular "new" type of whiskey called bourbon to settlers and Irish railroad workers. It was served from barrels that sat on the front porch of his store, which soon became known as the Bourbon Store. It did not take long before railroad workers began to identify the entire area as Bourbon, and the name stuck. In September 1853 a post office was established, and the town became known as Bourbon in the Village of St. Cloud. St. Cloud was the name of a proposed town that was to be located 1 1/2 miles to the east, but which never came to fruition.

With the coming of Highway 66 in 1926, auto courts, cafés, and service stations popped up all along the highway in this region. In 1932, six years following the designation of Highway 66, Alex and Edith Mortenson opened the Bourbon Lodge. The small, fledgling operation included a café and three overnight cabins. The café featured a 25-cent breakfast that included bacon, eggs, toast, and coffee, while a cabin, sans indoor plumbing, rented for a whopping 50 cents per night. A Phillips 66 station was later added, as was a fourth cabin. By 1939 the Mortensons were charging $1 to $1.50 per night for the cabins, which now included indoor toilets and showers. The Mortensons eventually sold the Bourbon Lodge in the early 1940s and moved a half mile west on Route 66, where they owned and operated the Hi Hill Cabins and Station until 1947.

Many of the Bourbon Lodge structures still stand today, including the lodge/café building that now serves as a private residence. The service station and a couple of cabins remain in varying states of disrepair. The people of Bourbon are proud of their small, friendly town and have no aspirations to become hurry-up, cold-hearted, "big city" people. They prefer instead to be known as plain folks who like to make you feel at home.

CUBA
c. 1936

Cuba had its beginnings in 1857 when two men, M. W. Trask and W. H. Ferguson, surveyed the town site in anticipation of the St. Louis & San Francisco Railway coming through the area. Responsibility for naming the town is said to have belonged to George Jamison and Wesley Smith. Smith suggested the name as a show of support for Cuban citizens, who were then under Spain's oppressive hold. Jamison wanted to name the town for his wife, Amanda, who had a post office already named for her just 1 1/2 miles west of the new proposed town site. Legend has it that the issue was resolved by standing a stick on end and letting it fall. How the stick landed determined the town's name.

The railroad played a vital role in the community's growth, and Cuba served as a major shipping point. Apples were another major factor in Cuba's developing economy until the early 1930s. When Highway 66 came through in 1926, things really began to explode, and by the 1930s the original town site was abandoned. Cuba moved away from the railroad tracks and closer to the new highway. It became a true highway town and much of its economy was based on the seemingly never-ending parade of tourist traffic. Motels, cafés, and service stations seemed to pop up overnight.

The interstate bypassed Cuba in the late 1960s, but the townspeople banded together to build a model community that is admired and emulated by many of Missouri's rural towns. The citizens of Cuba are proud of their Route 66 heritage. Large banners hanging from light poles and murals decorating Cuba's buildings celebrate the town's link to Route 66. Known as the "Gateway to the Ozarks" and the "Mural City," Cuba stands as a true Route 66 renaissance town and is a must-see when exploring the old road.

ROCK HAVEN CABINS, ST. JAMES
c. 1940

The Rock Haven is a classic example of a 1920s and early- 1930s motor court. These overnight rest stops provided simple, modest accommodations for tourists as well as traveling businessmen. Opened shortly after Highway 66 was designated a U.S. highway, the Rock Haven offered six small "modern" cabins built of native sandstone slabs known as giraffe rock. This rock was a common sight in the region and was used to build everything from homes and motels to filling stations and restaurants. Indoor plumbing was not typical of early motor courts and was, in fact, considered a luxury. The Rock Haven, like many original auto courts of the day, provided a community washhouse with hot and cold running water for showers.

In 1950 Frank and Ruth Waring purchased the Rock Haven and that summer added a wooden double cabin, a restaurant, and a new filling station that sold Standard Oil gasoline. In 1954 the Warings sold the business to Rudy Gilder, who operated the Rock Haven until the interstate bypassed it in the late 1960s. Converted to a nightclub and tavern in the 1970s, the restaurant building, although somewhat altered, is today a private residence. In 1988 all but one of the cabins were razed, leaving a small but tantalizing glimpse into the past of American auto travel and the halcyon days of Highway 66.

SCHUMAN'S TOURIST CITY, ROLLA
c. 1939

R. E. Schuman opened his "tourist city" in 1928, hoping to capitalize on the newly designated Highway 66 that ran through town. According to a quote from the *Rolla Herald* on June 27, 1929, "Seventeen clean comfortable cottages, ideally suited at the north city limits of Rolla, will cause thousands of tourists to stop in our city each season. It is a general comment of tourists that the Schuman Cottages are the nicest and cleanest along the highways."

Originally known as Schuman's Cottage City, then as Schuman's Tourist City, the business was known as Schuman's Motor Inn in the 1950s and 1960s. From the day the first cottages were completed in 1928, Schuman constantly made improvements to the guest units and to the grounds, adding conveniences such as covered parking, steam heat, radios, and telephones. By the late 1930s, Schuman's Tourist City also included a service station, café, and a two-story hotel with accommodations for 100 guests. The hotel was billed as offering "all

the facilities of a fine city hotel combined with the conveniences of an ultra modern motor court."

In 1931 an armed gunman held up Schuman's, leading the owners to hire a watchman to patrol the grounds at night. The patrolman carried a watch clock that he punched at designated stations throughout the grounds, covering "all parts of the court and all floors of the hotel," as the back of a period postcard states.

Schuman became a prominent businessman in the Rolla area and owned several other businesses, including the Central Missouri Hatchery that turned out thousands of baby chicks a week, and a commercial flower garden located adjacent to the motel. Surviving well into the 1960s as Schuman's Motor Inn, the former Tourist City eventually closed. Today its past is a distant, fading memory for thousands of tourists who made Schuman's a unique "city" unto itself as they made their way to untold destinations along Route 66.

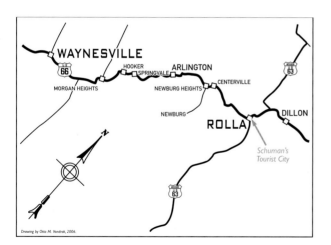

Drawing by Otto M. Vondrak, 2006.

PARTIAL VIEW, SCHUMAN'S TOURIST CITY, ROLLA. MO.

4 ACRE COURT, LEBANON
c. 1939

Ray Coleman and Blackie Walters built the 4 Acre Court in 1939 in the hopes of cashing in on the ever-increasing flow of traffic heading down Highway 66. To attract vacationing families, they built individual cabins with a fireplace in each. The cabins were "rocked" using the giraffe-stone exterior that was so popular in this region of the Ozarks during the 1930s and 1940s. For the more adventurous travelers, a campground was located to the west of the main building. This campground was eventually turned into a children's playground. A two-story building out front served as the owners' residence and office and at one time also housed a gas station and convenience store.

Today the one- and two-room cottages comprise an apartment complex called Village Oaks. In 2003 one of the cottages was destroyed by fire, but luckily none of the other remaining units were damaged.

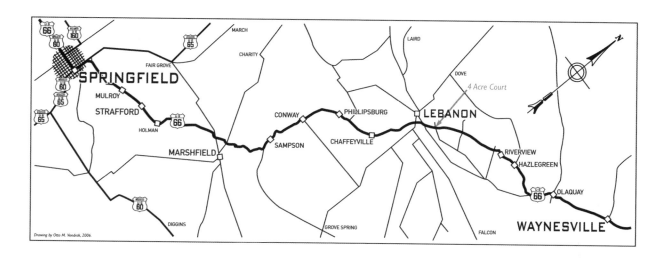

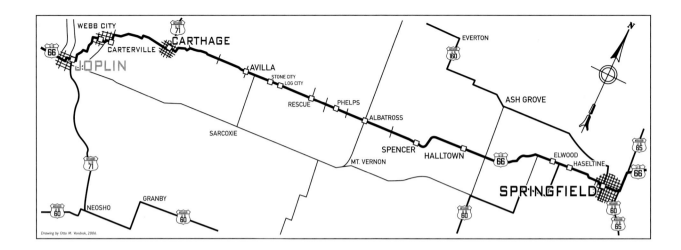

Drawing by Otto M. Vondrak, 2006.

JOPLIN
c. 1940s

Joplin holds the honor of being one of the 14 Route 66 cities forever immortalized in Bobby Troup's legendary hit song "Route 66." Located on the Ozark Plateau in the southwest corner of Missouri, just 200 miles from the geographical center of the country, Joplin was established in 1848 and was once known as the lead and zinc mining capital of the world. It was named for Reverend Harris G. Joplin, who founded the first Methodist Church in Jasper County in 1840. Because of its central location, Joplin became a major shipping point for many of the country's largest trucking companies.

Excessive mining has created many problems for the city, including a number of street cave-ins caused by the numerous abandoned mine tunnels under the city. As a result, Route 66 saw many alignment changes in Joplin over the years, including a City 66, Alternate 66, and a Bypass 66.

From 1979 to the route's demise in 1985, the Joplin area was designated the easternmost terminus of Route 66. During the glory days of the Mother Road, Main Street in downtown Joplin was a bustling and thriving entity lined with huge department stores, no less than 20 hotels, banks, eight movie houses, and every type of shop imaginable. Back during Joplin's rowdy mining days, an establishment called the House of Lords on Main Street advertised "fine cuisine, gambling and 'soiled doves.' " Today the site of the notorious House of Lords is a city park, and most of what was downtown Joplin long ago moved to outlying malls. A few cafés, taverns, and specialty shops still serve the downtown area, but most of these struggle to survive.

KANSAS

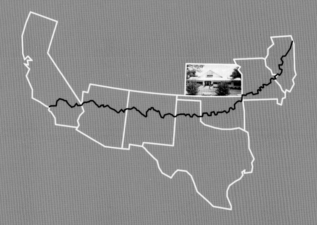

SPRING RIVER BRIDGE, RIVERTON
c. 1926

Built in 1922 by the Marsh Bridge Company, the Spring River Bridge was an elegant three-span structure designed by James B. Marsh, who began a professional career as a bridge designer with the King Bridge Company of Cleveland, Ohio, in 1883. During his tenure with the King Bridge Company, which was one of the largest in the United States at that time, Marsh also became the head of the Northern Agency for the Kansas City Bridge and Iron Company, where he not only was a key designer, but also oversaw construction.

By March 1889 Marsh had become general western agent and contracting engineer for the King Bridge Company and was placed in charge of the general western office in Des Moines, Iowa. In the spring of 1896 he formed his own company, the Marsh Bridge Company, and at the turn of the century began to design bridges utilizing a steel skeleton structure encased in concrete, which gave his bridges their unique and graceful look.

In April 1904 the Marsh Bridge Company was incorporated as the Marsh Engineering Company, and in 1912 Marsh was awarded a patent for the Marsh Rainbow Arch Bridge, a design that became a favorite with state engineers and county commissioners. The bridge could be built using inexpensive materials, and it was durable, aesthetically pleasing, and virtually maintenance free. A standard Marsh bridge consisted of one to three arches, although they have been built using as many as 11 arches. The earliest known Marsh bridge in Kansas was built in 1917, and the last was erected in 1934. Construction of the arch bridges reached its peak in the late 1920s and declined after 1930.

In 1986, too narrow to handle the modern traffic flow and simply obsolete, the Spring River Bridge was dismantled. The Willow Creek Bridge near Baxter Springs met its end on November 11, 1991. The only remaining Marsh bridge on Route 66 rests a couple of miles west of Riverton over Brush Creek. Built in 1923, the single-span Brush Creek Bridge was listed on the National Register of Historic Places in 1983. It was slated for demolition in the mid-1990s, but the combined preservation efforts of the Kansas Route 66 Association, the Cherokee County Commission, and protesters from around the world saved it. The Brush Creek Bridge was fully restored. Today it stands as a testament to its designer and as a memorial to the millions of motorists who traveled her during the glory days of the Mother Road.

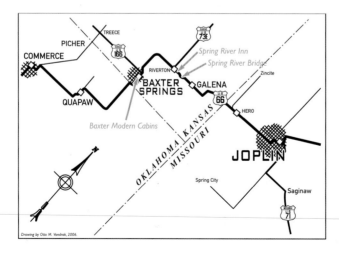

Drawing by Otto M. Vondrak, 2006.

SPRING RIVER INN, RIVERTON
c. 1960

Traveling westward just across the Spring River Bridge, one encountered the entrance to the historic Spring River Inn. In the early years of Missouri's statehood, this area along the banks of the Spring River was declared a no man's land and a no-fighting zone for Missouri citizens and the Cherokee nation. By 1869 this buffer zone was no longer necessary, and the land was opened to settlers.

In 1902 B. F. Steward built a private residence on a parcel of land along the edge of the Spring River and thus laid the groundwork for the Spring River Inn. On July 24, 1905, Steward sold his home to the Country Club of Joplin, Missouri. The club became the social center of the area and was so popular that it was a regular stop on the Joplin trolley line. In 1913 the Country Club boasted an early version of a built-in swimming pool known as a swimming tank. Only 4 feet deep, the pool's abandoned foundation still sits a few hundred yards northeast of the inn.

The Spring River Inn was situated on 7 1/2 acres and included tennis courts, picnic areas, and boating facilities. When the Great Depression hit in the 1930s, the club fell on hard times. In 1932 club president J. W. Grantham bought the building and used it for several years as a summer home for himself and his wife, Cora Pear. The Granthams regularly entertained theater celebrities there as actors made their way through Joplin and Baxter Springs on tour. After only a few years, however, the home stood vacant, abandoned and all but forgotten.

Thankfully the inn was purchased and saved by June and Gates Harrold in 1952. They fully converted the inn to a large restaurant with six private dining areas, including a room to seat over 350 guests. The Harrolds sold in 1970 and from then to 1994 Judy and Ray Birk owned and operated the Spring River Inn. On November 1, 1994, partners David and Kay Graham and Dewayne and Lavern Treece purchased the inn. The Spring River Inn was well known for its 35-foot all-you-can-eat buffet, a culinary delight loaded with delicious home-cooked food and desserts, including two trademark specialties: cinnamon pull-apart bread and squaw bread.

The Spring River Inn closed in 1996 and met its permanent demise in a fire that completely destroyed the building on October 20, 1998.

BAXTER MODERN CABINS, BAXTER SPRINGS
c. 1947

Built in the mid-1940s, this classic U-shaped motel consisted of 12 guest rooms and a gas station that doubled as the motel office. Each gable-roofed unit was connected to a covered carport that featured an unusual semicircle façade. Legend has it that two married lovers who were carrying on an illicit affair made the motel their usual meeting place. One evening a faulty natural gas line filled their room with gas, and they never awoke from their blissful sleep. They were found the next morning together in bed, much to the dismay of their respective spouses.

Highway 66 through Kansas comprised just slightly more than 13 miles of roadway, but provided a microcosm of the entire route. Service stations, cafés, and motels, as well as various stands and shops, were located all along those 13 miles. Most are long gone, as are the Baxter Modern Cabins, which closed around 1965. A faceless Wal-Mart now sits on the former site of the motel where travelers and the occasional star-crossed couple sought refuge. If you tend to believe in such things as ghosts, you have to wonder if the two lost souls, hopelessly in love, are endlessly wandering the store aisles searching for a way out.

OKLAHOMA

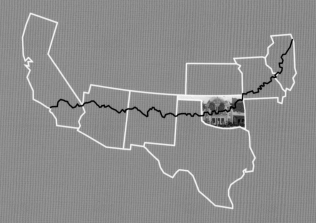

THE COLEMAN THEATER, MIAMI
c. 1939

The beautifully opulent Coleman Theater sits on Main Street in Miami, Oklahoma, on what was once Route 66. It was built in 1929 at a cost of $590,000 by George L. Coleman Sr., who made his fortune mining zinc and lead in the area. Coleman handed over the designing chores to the Boller Brothers of Kansas City, Missouri, who came up with the majestic Spanish-Colonial design, complete with hand-carved gargoyles and figurines. The interior is of Louis XV design and features gold-leaf trim, stained-glass windows, and carved mahogany railings and moldings.

Vaudeville was the entertainment of the time, and the Coleman opened to a sellout crowd on April 18, 1929. Patrons paid $1 each for admission. Since then, the Coleman has hosted many well-known performers, including Will Rogers and the infamous fan dancer Sally Rand. By the dawn of the 1940s, vaudeville had fallen out of favor, and the Coleman began showing the latest in motion pictures. In 1983 it was listed on the National Register of Historic Places, and it was donated to the city of Miami by the Coleman family in 1989. By 1990 movies were no longer shown at the Coleman except for the occasional revival classic. Friends of the Coleman was founded in 1992 to preserve the legacy of the theater and restore the Coleman to its original grandeur.

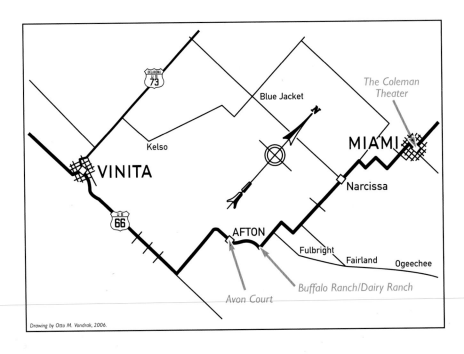

Drawing by Otto M. Vondrak, 2006.

BUFFALO RANCH/DAIRY RANCH, AFTON
c. 1959

Russell and Aleene Kay opened the Buffalo Ranch on July 11, 1953, after two years of searching for the perfect location to establish a tourist business. They eventually decided on this portion of land in northeast Oklahoma near Afton where Highways 69, 60, and 66 merged. From the beginning the couple decided to raise buffalo as part of their trading-post business. They opened the Ranch with a budget of $5,000 and seven head of bison. The business prospered over the next few years and grew with the addition of a Western store (billed as the world's largest), a barbecue restaurant, and an ice cream parlor. The Chuck Wagon barbecue restaurant accommodated 65 to 70 people; customers sat on benches at long tables and helped themselves to a family-style buffet. The Dairy Ranch ice cream parlor, which opened around 1954, served simpler fare, including burgers, fries, and ice cream treats. In 1958 the Dairy Ranch was purchased by Betty Wheatley, who ran the store until the end of the 2000 summer season.

Over the years the Buffalo Ranch became a very popular tourist stop, as thousands of travelers heading west jumped at the chance to stop and see the wild bison and purchase souvenirs. The Buffalo Ranch was most successful during the peak operating season, which lasted from Memorial Day to Labor Day. During that time the Buffalo Ranch sponsored Indian tribal dances to attract tourists. Most of the dancers lived in small huts on the property. Rabbits and chickens, as well as larger livestock such as llamas, elk, deer, sheep, and goats, were added to the menagerie, and the bison herd topped out at 40 head. There was never a charge to view the animals.

In 1963 Russell Kay passed away and left Aleene alone to operate the Buffalo Ranch. She admitted that it was a terrible struggle at first, but she persevered. The Will Rogers Turnpike (Interstate 44) bypassed Route 66 in this area in 1957, but the Buffalo Ranch complex held its ground and continued operating until Aleene's death in 1997. Sadly, the stock and furnishings were auctioned off on April 4, 1998, and the Buffalo Ranch was eventually bulldozed. A modern travel center now sits on the property. The new owner still calls the business the Buffalo Ranch and has even acquired a few buffalo in an effort to keep the legacy alive.

Avon Court
Hi-ways 69-66-60-59, Afton, Okla.
W. R. Trebilcock, Prop.

AVON COURT, AFTON
c. 1951

John Foley built the Avon Court in 1936 on the west end of the small town of Afton. It was a relatively small motel, consisting of just seven units. Each unit was built with its own covered carport, a common guest convenience for motels of that era. "Panel Ray Heat, Air Cooled, Clean, Comfortable Reasonable Rates and a Modern Trailer Park" were all part of the advertised amenities.

The Avon Court changed hands several times. At the time this postcard was made, it was owned and operated by W. R. Trebilcock, who bought the property in 1951 and operated it until 1955, when he sold it to Harry Glover. The interstate bypass was built in 1957, and in 1958 Glover sold the property. Although barren and empty, the skeletons of three units still stand today, providing a brief glimpse into a long-gone era.

During the heyday of Route 66, Afton was a beehive of activity, boasting several service stations, cafés, and motels. The bypass had a devastating impact on the town and its economy, making Afton an archetypal example of the damage done by the super slab.

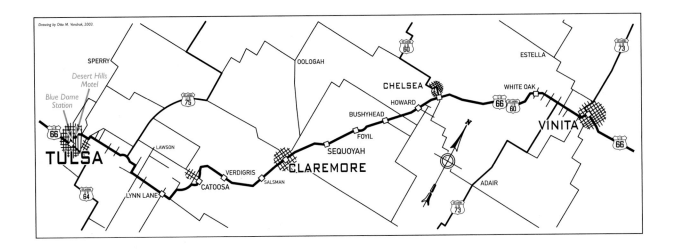

Drawing by Otto M. Vondrak, 2003.

DESERT HILLS MOTEL, TULSA
c. 1953

In 1933 the path of Highway 66 entering Tulsa from the east was routed down Eleventh Street, much to the delight of local businesses. Cafés, motels, and service stations sprang up along the entire stretch of Eleventh Street into downtown Tulsa. In 1953 the Desert Hills Motel and its often-photographed classic neon sign were erected just 10 minutes from downtown. The motel is set up in a U shape that consists of 50 units and an office. The motel boasted individually air-conditioned units, wall-to-wall carpeting, and free radio and television. Guests were also treated to free morning coffee served in the lobby. At one time the amenities included a pool, but it has long since been filled in.

By 1973 the Tulsa area and the Desert Hills Motel were completely bypassed, and the motel struggled to survive. What followed the bypass is a story similar to those of hundreds of motels along Route 66. As tourist traffic faded, rooms became weekly and monthly rental units, and dollars once spent on upkeep and maintenance became nonexistent.

In 1996 Jack Patel bought the Desert Hills Motel with a desire to restore it to its former glory. "When I bought the motel, only 25 rooms were in operating condition," he says. He meticulously renovated each room until all 50 were guest ready. For now the classic neon sign continues to light up Tulsa's evening sky, its warm inviting glow enticing rest-starved travelers to enjoy a quiet night's sleep within.

BLUE DOME STATION, TULSA
c. 1949

T. J. Chastain built the Blue Dome station in 1925 on the corner of Second Street and Elgin Avenue. Chastain was the owner and manager of the Chastain Oil Company, a large manufacturer and distributor of petroleum products in the Tulsa region, and the Blue Dome was his first effort to expand his business interests by adding retail outlets for his own Superoil products. A business associate suggested that the domes around the station be painted blue and the station be called the Blue Dome. Chastain did not take to the idea at first, but eventually changed his mind, and the name stuck.

The station originally sold and distributed Chastain's own Superoil products. But in 1928 Chastain procured the Tulsa County rights to Tydol Oil and sold Tydol Gasoline and Veedol Motor Oil alongside Superoil. Later on, Gulf Oil products were sold at the station.

The Blue Dome is said to be the first station in Oklahoma to provide such customer conveniences as hot water, pressurized air, and the until-then-unheard-of car wash. It was a huge success and one of the highest-grossing stations in the entire region, open 24 hours a day, 7 days a week. Upstairs in the dome itself, accessed by a spiral staircase, there was a small living space for the manager. In 1928 a second station was built at Fourth Street and Detroit Avenue. The original Blue Dome is being restored and is one of many Art Deco treasures found in the Tulsa area.

THE BLUE DOME, "BEST IN WEST", 2nd AND ELGIN, TULSA, OKLA. ~ 1949, ROUTE 66

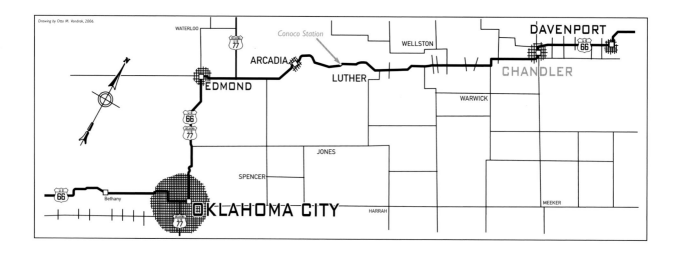

Drawing by Otto M. Vondrak, 2006.

CHANDLER
c. 1940

Named for U.S. Assistant Secretary of the Interior George Chandler, the town of Chandler was established in September 1891, when its first post office opened its doors. Six years later, a ferocious tornado ripped through the town, destroying most of the structures and killing 14 people. The town's citizens banded together and quickly began rebuilding Chandler. Twelve of the rebuilt structures are listed on the National Register of Historic Places, including the Wolcott Building (City Drug Store) and the St. Cloud Hotel, both on Manvel Avenue.

Chandler is also home to a 1930s-style Phillips 66 service station. Located at Seventh and Manvel, the station has been undergoing restoration for the past several years. Bill Fernau, the owner of the property, hopes not only to fully restore it but also to turn it into a working station.

William Tilgham served as sheriff of Chandler from 1901 to 1905 and was a deputy to Bat Masterson. Tilgham became a state senator in

1910 and returned to active duty as a sheriff in nearby Cromwell in 1924. On November 1 of that same year, he was killed in what is considered the last gunfight of the Old West. He was laid to rest in a local Chandler cemetery.

When Route 66 was designated to run through Chandler in 1926, Manvel Avenue, the town's main street, was paved with brick and was actually one of the few "hard" roads in the area. Oklahoma was then known for its vast, rich oil fields, and Chandler was regarded as the gateway into the state's oil country. Oil pumps, or "grasshoppers," are still a very common sight on Route 66 from Chandler west to Oklahoma City and beyond. This region is also known as pecan country. At one time so many pecans were grown here that Chandler was known as the "Pecan Capital of the World."

The Turner Turnpike (I-44) bypassed Chandler in 1953, but the townspeople took it in stride. Despite the setback, the community continued to grow and develop.

CONOCO STATION, ARCADIA
c. 1940

It is believed that this primitive stone station was built between 1915 and the very early 1920s. Its location was so remote that electricity was never run to the building. Kerosene lamps were used for lighting instead, compounding the dangers already involved in dispensing gasoline. The station also sold oil and kerosene, which were dispensed from large metal drums with only simple spigots to control the flow.

Local legend has it that the owners were involved in counterfeiting U.S. currency. Times were tough during the 1930s, so when a "salesman" paid a visit and offered a way to make a lot of quick cash, the temptation was too much. The story goes that the owners purchased a set of printing plates to make bogus $10 bills and even added a tiny room to the back of the station to serve as a print shop. The room was well disguised; its only entrance was a window on the back wall. Eventually the counterfeit bills were traced back to the station, where the plates were found, and the owners were arrested and sent to prison. The station was closed, never to open again. The stone ruins remain, seemingly daring time and the elements to take their best shot. My 10 bucks are on the stone.

KEY TOLL BRIDGE, GEARY
c. 1926

Built in 1921 over the South Canadian River, the Key Toll Bridge was named for its builder, local politician George D. Keys. Several predecessors to the Key Toll Bridge dated back to the late 1800s, but all met with disastrous ends, washed out by heavy rains and subsequent rushing high water. A high-water bridge was needed, and Keys was the man to get it done. The new suspension-style bridge swept 1,000 feet across the South Canadian River, connecting the towns of Geary and Bridgeport.

In November 1926 a jagged dirt road pathway from Calumet to Geary, as well as the bridge between Geary and Bridgeport, became parts of the new U.S Highway 66. Local support for the new highway was huge. Geary citizens were so enthused about the possibility of Highway 66 running through their town that hundreds volunteered to gravel and grade the road and thus ensure Geary's inclusion in the new highway. A free campground for travelers, sponsored and maintained by the Geary Businessmen's Club, was also built to attract business.

Despite public protest, the Key Bridge remained a toll crossing from its completion in 1921 until 1930. A tollbooth on the Geary side was manned and operated by William Phillips. He and his family lived on-site, and his wife sold sandwiches and snacks to passing motorists. Tolls ranged from 25 cents for horses to $1 for automobiles. A dollar was a steep price to pay in those days, but unless you were willing to travel 50 miles to the nearest reliable free crossing, you had no choice. Many a motorist was stranded when unable to pay the toll.

Continued protests rang loud. As a result, the bridge was purchased by the state of Oklahoma in 1930, and the toll was eliminated. Unfortunately for the citizens of Calumet, Geary, and Bridgeport, the utopia created by Highway 66 came to an early end. In October 1932 construction began on a new bridge 3 miles to the east of the Key Bridge. The new crossing would be part of a Highway 66 realignment that would bypass the three communities and connect El Reno and Hydro via a straight shot. On July 17, 1934, the El Reno Cut-Off was completed, and a reported 15,000 people attended a celebration at the new bridge.

The Key Bridge remained intact but was utilized for local traffic only. In 1946 fire severely damaged the Key Bridge and, due to costs, repair was out of the question. In 1952 the Key Bridge was sold to a Kansas City salvage company and was dismantled without fanfare shortly thereafter.

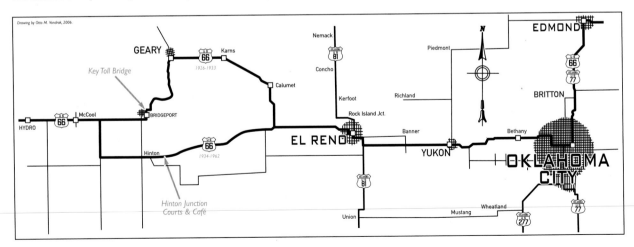

Drawing by Otto M. Vondrak, 2006.

HINTON JUNCTION COURTS & CAFÉ, HINTON JUNCTION

c. 1951

The Hinton Junction Café was built by E. B. Enze and was located just west of the pony-truss bridge that currently carries traffic over the South Canadian River. Officially known as the William H. Murray Bridge, the pony truss replaced the Key Toll Bridge when Highway 66 was rerouted away from Calumet, Geary, and Bridgeport in 1934.

Leon Little, who owned a succession of tourist facilities in the area, including a gas station near the Key Toll Bridge, moved this business when Highway 66 was rerouted. In 1943, after being drafted, Little leased his business to Enze. In a shrewd business move, Enze shut down Little's facility and opened a café and gas station of his own nearby. The lease was up soon after the war, and

Little and his wife, Ann, returned to pick up where they had left off, reopening their gas station and café.

Enze's business thrived during the late 1940s and 1950s, pumping gasoline 24 hours a day and serving food. A small motel with four rooms was added in a building at the back of the property. This motel portion of the business eventually expanded to include "ten modern cabins with individual air conditioning and television," as the back of the period postcard states. Business was great until traffic moved from Highway 66 onto the interstate in 1962. The number of cars traveling Route 66 dwindled to almost nothing, forcing the eventual closure of both Enze's Hinton Junction Courts and Café and Little's Gas Station and Café.

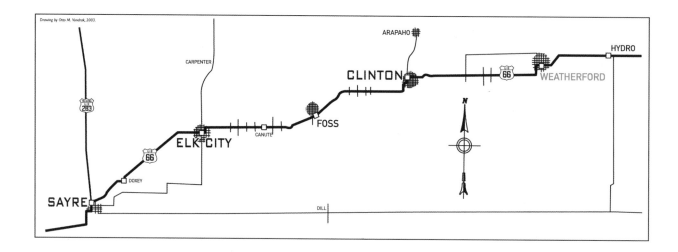

Drawing by Otto M. Vondrak, 2003.

WEATHERFORD, OKLAHOMA
c. 1952

On April 18, 1892, settlers began lining up at the western edge of Oklahoma's Cheyenne and Arapaho country in anticipation of the third Oklahoma land rush. One of these settlers, William J. Weatherford of Arkansas, settled his claim with his wife Lorinda, their four children, his widowed sister-in-law, and two hired hands. In an area that he called Jordan Flats, Weatherford built a five-bedroom house. In 1893 a post office was established in the house and Lorinda became its first postmistress.

In 1898 the Choctaw, Oklahoma & Gulf Railroad began its westward expansion and surprisingly located its terminus approximately 2 miles from the original Weatherford Settlement. On July 16, 1898, Beeks Erick, a local businessman, founded the location of current-day Weatherford and became town-site manager. Lots were sold and businesses, including a hotel and restaurant, were set up, albeit in tents. An application for a post office was sent to Washington, D.C., naming the new town Dewey,

but the application came back stating there was already a town named Dewey in the territory. The post office at the Weatherford home was closed and the new town was named Weatherford.

Weatherford was incorporated on May 2, 1898, and Erick became the first mayor. Weatherford quickly became known as a rough and bawdy frontier town. As many as 20 saloons were said to operate within 60 days of its founding. By 1905 temperance groups had helped cut the number of saloons to two.

Regular train service began on November 14, 1898, and turned Weatherford into a major rail hub. Herds of cattle were regularly driven down Main Street to the railroad stockyards. In November 1926 that same dirt Main Street became U.S. Highway 66. By the 1960s much of Route 66 in the area was a four-lane highway, but in June 1970 exits and entrances to Interstate 40 were completed on either side of town and Weatherford became another victim of the dreaded Interstate bypass.

TEXAS

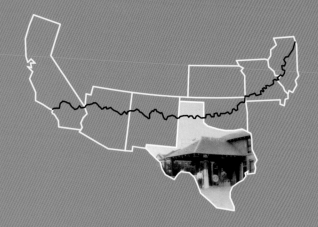

SHAMROCK
c. 1960

At the far eastern edge of the Texas Panhandle, about 15 miles from the Oklahoma border, sits the town of Shamrock. The earliest white settlers in the area were mostly buffalo hunters bent on eradicating the vast herds with the blessing of the U.S. government. Because hunters draped bison hides over their makeshift homes, the area initially became known as Hidetown.

The postal service awarded Shamrock a post office in 1880. George Nickel, an Irish immigrant, was its first postmaster and named the region for his homeland. The railroads arrived in 1902 and formally brought civilization to Shamrock.

Early U.S. Highway 66 through the Texas Panhandle comprised mostly primitive dirt roads that twisted and turned through desert prairies. Conditions were so bad that the 90-mile trip from Shamrock to Amarillo in good weather was expected to take about two full days.

By the mid-1930s, Route 66 ran down Twelfth Street on the north side of town, and Shamrock began to grow like wildfire. In the later part of the decade, service stations, cafés, and auto courts sprang up everywhere along the strip, and in 1937 thousands attended a parade to celebrate the paving of Highway 66 through town. By the late 1960s, however, construction of the new interstate was progressing, and in 1972 the town of Shamrock was cut off by the new I-40.

Neon lights from the dozens of cafés, service stations, and auto courts once lit the evening skies and could be seen from as far as twenty miles away. Today, the "Little Las Vegas" strip is just a fading memory, and only a handful of businesses remain. Much of the neon and glitz along this stretch of highway has quietly faded into the emptiness of the Texas desert landscape.

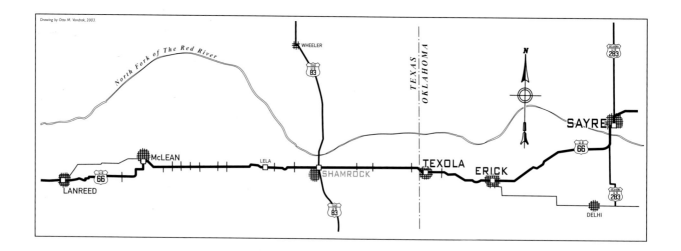

Drawing by Otto M. Vondrak, 2003.

GOLDEN SPREAD GRILL, GROOM
c. 1958

Groom is located 42 miles east of Amarillo. It was named for the first general manager of the Francklyn Land and Cattle Company, B. B. Groom, and laid out in 1902 on the route of the Rock Island Railway. The 1920s brought an oil boom to the area, which, coupled with the new Highway 66, increased the town's population to 564 residents by 1931.

As oil production faded, agriculture and the tourist trade became the mainstays of the local economy. The Golden Spread Grill opened in 1957 and was one of four restaurants enjoying successful business in town. Soon after it opened, Ruby Denton took over the business and made the Golden Spread Grill a very popular eatery for travelers as well as locals. The back of the advertising postcard reads, "Always stop at the Golden Spread and be among the best fed." People did stop, and the restaurant's popularity grew.

Business boomed until one day in June 1980, when Interstate 40 bypassed Groom and crushed many of the town's roadside businesses. Today the structure that was once the Golden Spread Grill still stands and continues to serve travelers as the Route 66 Steakhouse.

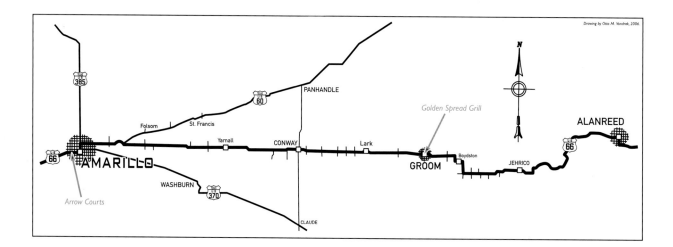

Drawing by Otto M. Vondrak, 2006.

ARROW COURTS, AMARILLO
c. 1955

By 1927 Amarillo was well on its way to becoming a popular tourist town. Motorists flocked into town via Highways 66, 60, 87, and 287—four major arteries that provided local roadside tourist stops with all the business they could handle. So great was the influx of visitors from the burgeoning auto/tourist trade that as many as 29 Amarillo auto courts and camps competed for the tourist dollar in 1927.

The Arrow Courts, later known as the Arrow Motel, were located on the western edge of greater Amarillo and were actually considered to be outside of the city limits. It was a good place to stop if you were traveling west and wanted to miss the city's morning traffic or the hustle and bustle of Amarillo's "Motel Row," located on the east side on Eighth Street. The Arrow's guest rooms were located in two buildings, one with four units and one with eight. An island courtyard filled with plants and trees lay parallel to the eight-unit building, forming a driveway with parking in front of each room. An office building located at the front of the property doubled as a gas station but provided no garage service. A café/restaurant unaffiliated with the motel was conveniently situated just west of the office. The Arrow Motel provided guests with panel-ray heat, carpeted floors, and tile baths. Owners and operators Mr. and Mrs. O. E. Allen (circa 1955) proclaimed the Arrow Motel to be "a clean, quiet place for a good night's rest."

In 1968 Interstate 40 bypassed the city and relegated Route 66 to I-40 business-loop status. In 1985, Highway 66 was decertified and left for dead. The Arrow Courts property is currently a private residence.

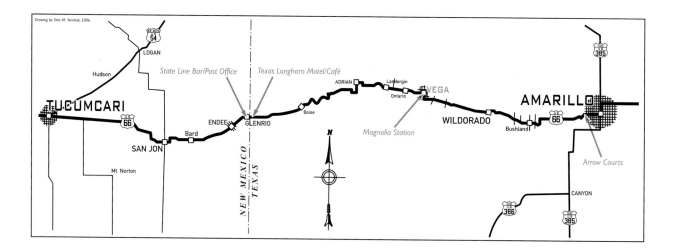

Drawing by Otto M. Vondrak, 2006.

VEGA
c. 1959

The small town of Vega, Texas, sits quietly along old Highway 66 about 30 miles west of Amarillo. Vega, Spanish for "grassy meadow," had its beginnings in 1897 when the state of Texas opened up the land in the area for homesteading. On October 17, 1899, early settler N. J. Whitfield purchased what would become the town site for $1 an acre. In May 1903 A. Miller and Howard Trigg surveyed the area, and Miller opened the first general store in Vega later that year. The following year a post office, saloon, and school were built, solidifying the fledgling community. A bank was established in 1908, and in 1909 the Choctaw, Oklahoma & Gulf Railroad (later the Rock Island) was completed, bolstering the town's economy. By 1915 Vega's population grew to 223.

Prior to 1926 the Old Ozark Trail carried the first automobile traffic through town. When Highway 66 was commissioned in 1926, the new highway followed along the original dirt pathway of the Ozark Trail through Vega. As automobile travel grew in popularity, tourist courts, service stations, and cafés were built all along the town's main street. By 1937 the highway was paved and realigned through town.

Vega was one of the last towns in Texas to see the Interstate 40 bypass, but by the late 1970s the inevitable was completed. Many early buildings still stand on both alignments of Route 66 through town, including the Magnolia Station, which dates to the early 1920s. The Vega Motel, an original tourist court, is also still in operation (see the first *Route 66 Lost & Found*).

Howdy from Vega, Texas

MAGNOLIA STATION, VEGA
c. 1926

The Magnolia Station was built in 1924 by "Colonel" J. T. Owen on a lot he purchased in 1923, when the primitive dirt highway in front of it was known as the Ozark Trail. The Magnolia Station was the second service station built in Vega during the 1920s. By the time Highway 66 came through town, Edward and Cora Wilson had leased the Magnolia from Owen. The Wilsons lived above the station until 1930, when the Magnolia was leased to E. B. Cooke, who operated it for a short time before A. B. Landrum took over the lease in 1931.

In 1933 Owen's son Austin took over day-to-day operations at the station. He entered into a lease with the Phillips Petroleum Company, which charged him one cent per gallon of gasoline sold.

The highway directly in front of the Magnolia remained a dirt road during the time it served as Highway 66. By 1937 Route 66 was paved and realigned through Vega just south of the station, bypassing the downtown area. The Magnolia Station continued to provide gasoline until it shut down its pumps and ceased operation in 1953. The station was then used as a barbershop until 1965. It remained empty until the town of Vega and the Oldham County Chamber of Commerce restored it with partial funding from the Route 66 Corridor Preservation Program.

TEXAS LONGHORN MOTEL, CAFÉ AND SERVICE STATION, GLENRIO

c. 1950

Scared away in 1946 by talk of a new interstate that was being built through Glenrio, local businessman Homer Ehresman and family packed their bags and moved to Plainview, Texas. As 1950 came around, this new interstate seemed to be stuck on the drawing table, so Ehresman, with family in tow, returned to Glenrio and built the Texas Longhorn Motel, Café and Service Station on the Texas side of town. The business ran smoothly until the Rock Island Railroad closed its depot in 1955, handing Glenrio a sharp economic blow.

But the knockout punch was still many years to come. Ehresman's business struggled for a period, but tourist traffic eventually flourished and the business grew. The Longhorn's iconic "First/Last Stop In Texas" sign grew from a simply painted board to a giant illuminated billboard beckoning travelers to stop for a bite and spend the night. This enterprise remained highly successful for

Ehresman until the dawn of the 1970s. The interstate that had been staved off for decades now spelled economic doom for Glenrio and its businesses. The enterprising Ehresman, down but not out, built a new, modern motel and restaurant just 5 miles west of Glenrio, on the north side of the interstate's Endee exit.

It is a bit ironic that the last few guests of Ehresman's Texas Longhorn Motel were the construction workers building his new motel. The First/Last Stop In Texas complex closed for good by 1975, and the "new" motel now lies in ruins. Glenrio, now a legitimate ghost town, sits quiet and alone. Route 66, its main street, once hectic and alive, has transformed into a tumbleweed highway with only a casual stray dog to interrupt the monotony. The towering, beaconlike sign, once brightly lit and beckoning travelers, slowly disintegrates with each passing year.

NEW MEXICO

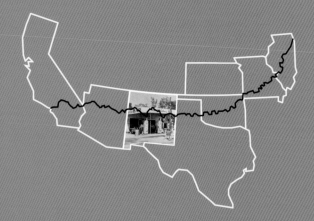

STATE LINE
BAR/POST OFFICE, GLENRIO
c. 1943

Founded in 1903, two years after the Rock Island Railroad wound its way through the area, Glenrio quickly grew through the 1920s as an agricultural and farming community. The name Glenrio stems from the English word *glen* meaning "valley" and the Spanish word *rio* meaning "river," though Glenrio is neither in a valley nor near a river. Glenrio straddles the Texas–New Mexico border, but the post office is in New Mexico. This caused confusion early on, because the mail was delivered to a depot on the Texas side of town. Connected to the post office was the State Line Bar, which was operated on the New Mexico side of town because Deaf Smith County on the Texas side was dry. The fact that the post office and bar are connected makes one wonder if the mail was ever delivered on time.

Highway 66 was still a dirt pathway through town when Homer Ehresman and his wife, Margaret, first arrived in Glenrio around 1934. The Ehresmans quickly went into business operating a service station, bar, and tourist court, while Margaret also ran the post office. By the fall of 1937 the dirt pathway running through Glenrio was finally paved. During the construction that ran from summer to fall, workers camped in tents alongside the road. By 1946 talk of a new interstate that would bypass Glenrio prompted the Ehresman family to pull up stakes (see the Texas chapter).

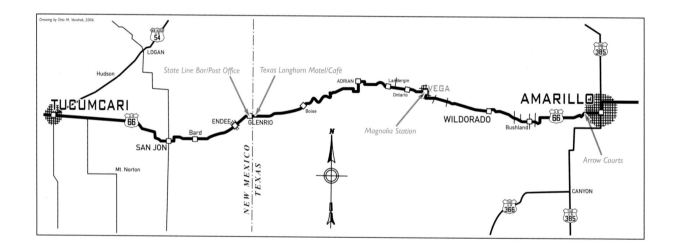

FLYING C RANCH, PALMA
c. 1945

Located 77 miles east of Albuquerque, near a speck of a town called Palma, the Flying C Ranch was built in 1945 by Roy Cline, who is more widely known for establishing Cline's Corners in 1933. In 1939 Cline sold the very successful Cline's Corners and moved on to Kingman, Arizona. After a few additional pit stops, he returned once again to eastern New Mexico, where he built the Flying C Ranch.

The Flying C Ranch featured a garage complete with wrecker, a filling station selling Texaco gas, and a small café. Much of the Flying C Ranch's business came from stranded motorists unaccustomed to traveling the Southwest's desert during the hot summer months. After completing a few stucco repairs, Cline's son painted one of the buildings stark white. The color attracted customers, and soon all the buildings were painted white. The Flying C developed into an all-purpose travel center when it became a regular stop for the Greyhound bus line.

Cline owned and operated the Flying C Ranch until 1963. Both Cline's Corners and the Flying C Ranch remain in business today without the involvement of any Cline family members. The Flying C is currently owned and operated by Bowlin Travel Centers Incorporated. The Bowlins have been meeting the needs of the traveling public since 1912, when Claude M. Bowlin began trading with Native Americans of New Mexico. The Bowlins currently own and operate 12 travel centers, all located in the Southwest, three of them on Historic Route 66. Each full-service travel center offers gifts, souvenirs, exclusive handmade Indian jewelry, and gasoline. Many also feature Dairy Queen restaurants. In 1972 Bowlin's youngest son, Michael L. Bowlin, became president and CEO of the operation and remains in charge to this day. Claude M. Bowlin died in 1974.

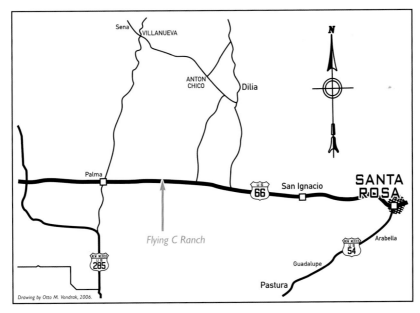

Drawing by Otto M. Vondrak, 2006.

LONGHORN RANCH MOTEL, MORIARTY
c. 1950

Located 70 miles west of Santa Rosa, the Longhorn Ranch Motel was a later addition to the landmark Longhorn Ranch complex. The Longhorn Ranch was built by one-time police officer Captain Eric Erickson, who began his business as a café with a few stools and a single counter. The wide-open desert between Santa Rosa and Albuquerque was barren and often harsh, with few tourist facilities along the way—the perfect scenario for the successes of tourist meccas like Cline's Corners, the Flying C Ranch, and the Longhorn Ranch. After World War II these outpost businesses expanded like wildfire. The Longhorn Ranch soon became an institution on Route 66, and travelers made it a point to stop there year after year.

At its peak the Longhorn Ranch included a café, garage, service station, curio shop, museum, cocktail lounge, restaurant, and motel. The motel was built on the north side of Highway 66, directly across from the main complex. It featured 15 ranch-style units and an office built to resemble a Western ranch house. The ranch-type setting was the perfect complement to the Old West theme that permeated the main complex across the highway. According to the period postcard, a night's rest at the Longhorn Ranch Motel was "air cooled by Nature" and offered rubber-foam mattresses and a café just "across the highway with one of the finest Dining Rooms and Cocktail Lounges on Highway 66."

Nothing but memories remain of the main Longhorn Ranch complex. So thorough was the demolition that one would be hard-pressed to even prove that the landmark roadside stop ever existed. The motel units survive, however, and provide a small taste of what a visit to one of the largest and most glamorous tourist facilities on Route 66 was like. If you decide to stop at the motel, take some time and walk across the old highway to the one-time site of the main Longhorn Ranch complex. If you stand very still, you might hear the sound of the ranch's famous Concord stagecoach whizzing by as Hondo the driver barks out orders to his team of horses.

CENTRAL AVENUE, ALBUQUERQUE
c. 1950

The Spanish villa of Albuquerque was founded in 1706 on the banks of the Rio Grande by Don Francisco y Valdes, the governor of New Mexico. The villa was named for the Duke of Alburquerque, the viceroy of New Spain, and as a result is sometimes referred to as the "Duke City." (The first *r* in Alburquerque was eventually dropped.) A vital stop on the *El Camino Real* or "King's Highway" connecting Mexico City to Santa Fe, the settlement grew quickly. In 1879 the Atchison, Topeka & Santa Fe Railway steamed into the area and established New Albuquerque about 1 1/2 miles east of what is now called Old Town. The following year, on April 22, the first rail passengers pulled into the new boomtown.

When Highway 66 was designated in 1926, the road passed through town via Fourth Street, crossed the Barelas Bridge, and continued down Isleta Boulevard. In 1937 the Santa Fe Loop was bypassed, and Route 66 traveled into town via Central Avenue.

Prior to realignment in 1935, only 3 tourist camps were located on Central Avenue, while 16 were in operation on Fourth Street. Four years after the realignment, Central Avenue became the focus of tourist facilities. Roadside development flourished, and the number of motels increased to 37.

After World War II and the end of gasoline rationing, the country once again looked to the automobile for vacation travel. By 1955, 98 motels were located on Route 66 within the city limits of Albuquerque. The vintage buildings and motels along the older Fourth Street alignment and the newer Central Avenue alignment represent a virtual museum of popular architectural styles utilized during Route 66's heyday out West, from Pueblo Revival to Southwest Vernacular to Streamline Moderne. Of the 98 motels operating along Central Avenue during Route 66's peak years, about 40 that date prior to 1955 still exist today. In 1970 Albuquerque was entirely bypassed by Interstate 40.

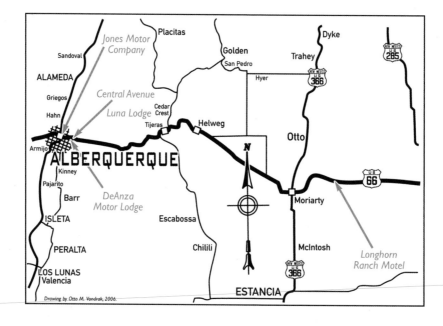

Drawing by Otto M. Vondrak, 2006.

WEST CENTRAL AVE.
ALBUQUERQUE, NEW MEXICO

LUNA LODGE, ALBUQUERQUE
c. 1949

In 1949 Route 66 through Albuquerque was called East Central Avenue, and one of the easternmost motels along this stretch was the Luna Lodge. Built in the Southwestern Vernacular style, the Luna Lodge originally consisted of three one-story white stucco buildings arranged in a broken U shape. The office and manager's residence were located at the front of the westernmost building. Deluxe rooms, which featured carports, were located in the west wing.

The Luna Lodge began operation by offering 18 rooms. By the late 1950s that number grew to 32, when the carports were converted to rooms and a second story was added to the west wing. The manager's apartment was moved to the front of the new second-story addition, and a porch that was once over the office was filled in to expand the residence. A café called the La Nortenita was also added as a separate structure to the front of the east wing during the 1950s.

Current owner Suresh Patel has owned the property since 1981. He leased the property to another operator from 1992 to 1997, but canceled the lease when that person did not maintain the property to his liking. In 1998 the Luna Lodge was listed on the National Register of Historic Places.

In 1979 Patel was employed at the New York State Department of Health. During an employee strike he was asked to take a job at a nearby nursing home. It was during this time that he realized how much he enjoyed helping people. Today many of Patel's guests at the Luna are older military veterans, whom he assists with doctor appointments and transportation to the nearby veterans' hospital. The monthly rent includes two meals a day at the motel's café. Buildings' facades may change and their original uses may become varied and confused, but the giving spirit of the road is alive and well at the Luna Lodge.

DE ANZA MOTOR LODGE, ALBUQUERQUE
c. 1939

C. G. Wallace and partner S. D. Hambaugh built the 30-unit De Anza Motor Lodge in 1939 in response to the growing number of motorists traveling the 1937 Highway 66 alignment through Albuquerque. The De Anza was named for Spanish Lieutenant Juan Batista de Anza, who rescued the Hopi pueblo from certain starvation and went on to serve as territorial governor of New Mexico from 1778 to 1788.

Unlike the smaller auto courts of the day, the De Anza sits on a full city block (2.5 acres) in the famous Nob Hill–Highland area along East Central Avenue. In 1939 the motel was the largest to date along that section of Central Avenue. The motor lodge was constructed in the popular Spanish–Pueblo Revival style and originally consisted of eight separate stucco buildings. Six one-story buildings formed the classic U-shaped motel of the period. Two two-story buildings, situated one behind the other, formed an island in the middle of the courtyard and served as the office and manager's residence. Each guest unit had a carport, all of which were eventually converted to more guest units.

In the decade following World War II, Wallace expanded the facility first to 55 units and then to 67 units. By 1957 a coffee shop and pool were added to meet the growing demands of the motoring public. The De Anza was such a popular stopover during its heyday that Wallace would regularly pick up and drop off VIPs at the airport in a shiny pink Cadillac. The De Anza remained listed as an American Automobile Association–approved accommodation until the early 1990s, and Wallace owned the motel until his death in 1993. It was subsequently sold and resold, eventually falling into a mild state of disrepair. Current owner Amir Naggi closed the doors in 2003.

The De Anza Motor Lodge was listed on the National Register of Historic Places on April 30, 2004. A local community redevelopment group is currently working with the City of Albuquerque to preserve and rehabilitate the property. They hope to maintain the integrity of this site, which is closely related to the history of tourism and Indian trade along the once-bustling highway.

THE NEW
DE ANZA
MOTOR LODGE
ALBUQUERQUE, NEW MEXICO

4301 EAST CENTRAL AVENUE, U. S. HIGHWAY NO. 66, 4 MILES EAST OF CITY CENTER

JONES MOTOR COMPANY, ALBUQUERQUE
c. 1943

In 1939 Ralph Jones built the Tom Danahy–designed structure that housed the Jones Motor Company. Hoping to meet the needs of the modern auto owner and traveler, Jones later incorporated a Texaco gas station, creating a Ford dealership and repair center all under one roof. Sitting on a prime location on the east side of town, the auto-repair station was one of the first encountered by westbound travelers on Highway 66.

One of the most notable characteristics of the Streamline Moderne–style building is the stepped tower, which is adorned with ornamental molding that underscores the tower's shape. The tower was centrally located over the main portion of the building and housed the service station's restrooms. In 1946 an additional showroom was added to the west side of the building to mirror the original showroom. During the 1950s, a paint and body shop was added in a separate structure to the south of the gas station.

During the Jones Motor Company's early years, many of the repairs done were on vehicles being driven out West by people fleeing the Dust Bowl. These vehicles were so loaded down with family possessions that access to broken parts was difficult at best. Jones built a long carport along the southern wall of the garage so that cars and trucks could be unloaded in the shade, thus making the vehicles more accessible for repair.

Jones was born on a cattle ranch in Wyoming, where he spent most of his early years. At the end of World War I cattle prices began to plummet, and, desperately needing to supplement his income, Jones took a job selling Model T Fords in Cheyenne. In 1928 he opened his first Ford dealership in Springer, New Mexico. That dealership was eventually moved to the Central Avenue location in Albuquerque and reopened as the Jones Motor Company.

Jones was a huge advocate of Highway 66 and was onetime president of the Route 66 Association, as well as president of the Albuquerque Chamber of Commerce and chairman of the New Mexico State Highway Department during the mid- and late 1940s. The business moved in 1957, and in the subsequent decades the building changed hands several times. The structure housed several businesses, including an army surplus store, a paint and body shop, and a moped dealership. In 1993 the Jones Motor Company building was listed on the National Register of Historic Places. In 1999 it was purchased by Dennis and Janice Bonfantine and lovingly brought back to life as a brewpub and restaurant called Kelley's Brewery. Great efforts were made to return the structure to its original design, including the preservation of the vintage garage doors and the addition of two classic Texaco gas pumps out front.

ARROW-HEAD CAMP, GLORIETA
c. 1926

The Arrow-Head Camp was located 22 miles east of Santa Fe on the original alignment of old Highway 66. The road through this area follows the path of the old Santa Fe Trail and is rich with wonderfully historic tales of the Old West. Here the Santa Fe Trail eventually developed into the National Old Trails Highway, Highway 66, and, presently, New Mexico Highway 50. The ancient road in front of the Arrow-Head Camp has seen the gamut of transportation over the last 150 years or so, from horse and wagon to big rigs.

The Arrow-Head Camp was quite a large facility for its time and included a store, cabins, campground, and gas station. During the 1930s the cost for an overnight stay in one of the cabins was 50 cents. Later in the 1940s, the Arrow-Head Camp became known as

Arrowhead Lodge and was a popular spot among locals for dinner and dancing. The camp, which comprised mostly log cabin structures, was also a favorite among tourists and sportsmen, situated as it was in a highly wooded, picturesque area.

Route 66's Santa Fe Loop through Glorieta saw service from November 11, 1926, until January 1937, when a new routing of the road straight from Santa Rosa to Albuquerque shaved off about 90 miles of New Mexico Route 66 roadway. Today the wooded setting that made the camp so scenic is slowly overtaking the log structures. Long ago the Arrow-Head Camp began the process of blending in with the neighboring trees and brush. One day, the camp will complete its journey and totally succumb to its surroundings.

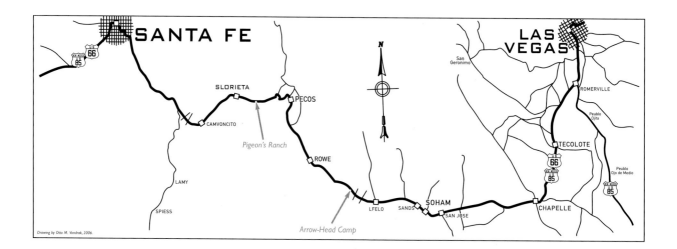

PIGEON'S RANCH, GLORIETA
c. 1929

Frenchman Alexander Valle built Pigeon's Ranch in the early 1820s, around the time that the Santa Fe Trail was being blazed. The name came from the fact that Valle spoke "pigeon English," or broken English, with a heavy French accent. The ranch became a very important site along the Santa Fe Trail, serving as a stagecoach stop, U.S. post office, and trading post.

On March 28, 1862, Pigeon's Ranch and the surrounding area, known as Glorieta Pass, was the site of the biggest and bloodiest battle of the Civil War in the Southwest. The adobe building shown here is said to have been used as a field hospital during that battle.

In 1924 Thomas "Tommie" Greer acquired the ranch and turned it into a roadside tourist attraction. Greer was a controversial figure, said to always be looking for a way to turn a buck. The stories go that he lured tourists to stop by offering to fill their jugs with free cold, pure mountain water. That gave him an opportunity to convince them to tour the historic battlefield—for a small fee, of course. Greer also claimed that the well on Pigeon's Ranch was the oldest in the United States. This claim was unfounded, but it made for good publicity. Bears were also part of this historic roadside attraction's allure; one particularly ornery black bear constantly harassed tourists and gave Greer trouble.

The bears were gone by the mid-1940s, and in 1966 Glorieta Pass Battlefield, upon which Pigeon's Ranch sits, was listed on the National Register of Historic Places. Today, the one remaining historically significant building on Pigeon's Ranch sits precariously close to NM 50—one wayward vehicle and the irreplaceable structure would be, shall we say, history. NM 50 also slices through the Glorieta Battlefield, making public access to the Civil War site difficult and dangerous. Strong efforts are being made to reroute NM 50 around the battlefield and to restore the area to its Santa Fe Trail and Civil War–era appearance.

LA BAJADA HILL, LA BAJADA
c. 1926

The origins of this infamous hill go back more than 400 years, when it was known as the *Camino Real de Tierra Adentro* and used as a footpath and wagon trail. The U.S. military began to regularly use La Bajada Hill ("the descent" in Spanish) after the Civil War. Soon the wagon road became the main route from Santa Fe to Albuquerque and was used by all types of traffic, including commercial stagecoach lines.

By 1910 adventurous automobile drivers were navigating the old wagon ruts, and in the early 1910s the state highway engineer ordered improvements to the road. Rock retaining walls and a new gravel surface improved the road somewhat. In the 1920s the road, by then known as National Old Trails Highway, was rerouted at the top end of the climb to make travel safer. On November 11, 1926, this portion of the road officially became U.S. Highway 66. From 1926 to 1932 the mere mention of La Bajada Hill struck terror in the hearts and minds of Route 66 motorists. The descent snaked 1.4 miles down the hill at a 6 percent grade and an elevation drop of over 500 feet. This, coupled with hazardous switchbacks, rattled the composure of many motorists. Ascending the hill, you had other worries. In the early days of the automobile fuel tanks were mounted above the carburetors. The ascent was so steep that many automobiles had to travel up the hill in reverse to allow fuel to feed the carburetor.

In 1932 Highway 66 was routed 3 miles east to the same route currently used by Interstate 25. Today, after 50-plus years of erosion and neglect, La Bajada is only traversable with high-clearance four-wheel-drive vehicles.

RIO PUERCO
TRADING POST, RIO PUERCO
c. 1940

The Rio Puerco Trading Post was first built in the early 1940s by George Thomas Hill Jr. and his wife, Morene, 19 miles west of Albuquerque, on the south side of the post-1937 realignment of Highway 66. A fire destroyed the original trading post, and the process of rebuilding began in 1946. The updated trading post burned in the 1960s and was replaced by a new enterprise owned by the Bowlin Corporation, the same company that owns the Flying C Ranch site and many other roadside facilities in the Southwest.

Every trading post needed a gimmick, and the Rio Puerco was no exception. A full-sized stuffed polar bear standing in a glass case greeted visitors as they entered the building. One night someone broke into the trading post, broke the glass case, and made off with the bear. It was later found ripped to shreds in the Sandi Mountains outside of Albuquerque.

The Rio Puerco is home to a historically significant bridge that was preserved by the New Mexico State Highway Department. The Parker Bridge, a through truss that spanned 250 feet over the often-treacherous Rio Puerco, was fabricated by the Kansas City Structural Steel Company and completed in 1933. The bridge helped to further the cause for the much-sought-after 1937 realignment of Highway 66 that bypassed Isleta and Los Lunas. The bridge no longer handles vehicle traffic, but can be crossed and explored on foot.

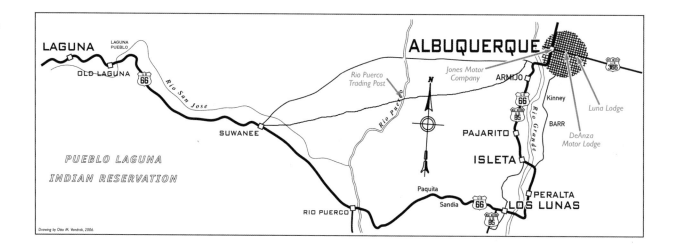

Drawing by Otto M. Vondrak, 2006.

ARIZONA

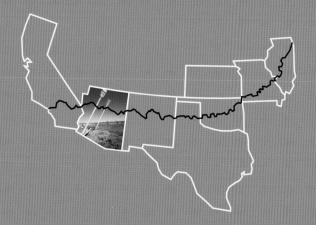

INDIAN TRAILS
TRADING POST, LUPTON
c. 1947

During the heyday of Highway 66, service stations, curio shops, and trading posts dotted the western stretch of "America's Main Street." Among the most colorful were four establishments located along the state line between New Mexico and Arizona: the State Line Trading Post, Fort Chief Yellowhorse, the Box Canyon Trading Post, and, perhaps the most popular, the Indian Trails Trading Post.

Max and Amelia Ortega established the Indian Trails Trading Post in 1946. In the beginning, local Navajo business was the mainstay, but Max soon expanded the small trading post into a full-service travel stop. As the business grew, the Ortega name became synonymous with fine handcrafted Indian jewelry, and to this day son Armond continues to be one of the largest Indian jewelry dealers in the world. Armond also went on to purchase and revitalize the landmark El Rancho Motel in nearby Gallup, New Mexico.

Today a handful of the old trading posts, including Fort Chief Yellowhorse, remain open, but only memories of the Indian Trails Trading Post remain. In 1965 Interstate 40 was completed from the New Mexico border to a few miles west of Lupton. The land where Indian Trails once sat is now an access road to a rest stop.

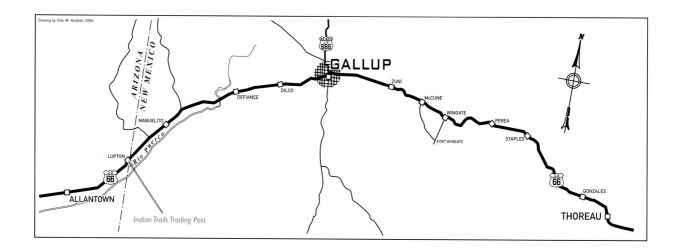

Drawing by Otto M. Vondrak, 2006.

505 INDIAN TRAIL TRADING POST — MAX ORTEGA TRADER — LUPTON, ARIZONA

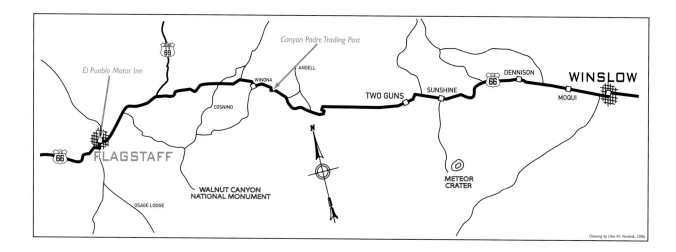

Drawing by Otto M. Vondrak, 2006

CANYON PADRE
TRADING POST, TWIN ARROWS
c. 1949

If you were looking for the quintessential Route 66 tourist stop, the Canyon Padre Trading Post would have to be a front runner in the voting. The Canyon Padre Trading Post was built in the late 1940s and consisted of a store, gas station, and café. The café was a small, 10-stool diner designed by the Valentine Manufacturing Company. Such prefabricated diners were very popular during the 1940s and 1950s and can still be found throughout the United States.

Sometime during the 1950s the Canyon Padre Trading Post became the Twin Arrows Trading Post. To catch the eye of passing motorists, two brightly painted arrows, each 20 feet high, were placed alongside the main building. Made from old telephone poles, the arrows are one of the most frequently photographed sights along all of Highway 66 and are icons of roadside architecture. The Twin Arrows was even featured in a car commercial in the mid-1990s.

A wide variety of goods were available in the trading post, including Navajo rugs, moccasins, and jewelry. When the interstate came through in the late 1960s, an exit to the Twin Arrows saved it from certain demise. The trading post closed in the early 1990s, but in 1995 it was reborn with the help of Spence and Virginia Reidel. Advertised as "The BEST 'Little' Stop on I-40," the post once again featured shelves stocked with souvenirs and pumps dispensing gasoline. Unfortunately, this rebirth did not last, and the business has remained closed since the late 1990s. The property has been severely neglected and is currently in an advanced state of disrepair. The twin arrows that once attracted camera-ready tourists from around the globe now stand beaten and worn, sadly marking the end of an era.

FLAGSTAFF
c. 1950

Settlers began arriving in what is now the Flagstaff area around 1876, and sheepherder Thomas Forsythe MacMillan is commonly credited as the area's first permanent resident. Legend has it that on July 4, 1876, settlers stripped a giant Ponderosa pine and raised an American flag in honor of the nation's centennial. Subsequently, they named the area "Flag Staff," and upon the opening of the post office in 1881 the town became known as Flagstaff. A year later the Atlantic & Pacific Railroad rolled into town, securing the town's future.

Fire destroyed the settlement in 1886 and 1888, but it was quickly rebuilt in both instances. In 1894 Dr. Percival Lowell was attracted to Flagstaff by its clear skies and established the world-famous Lowell Observatory, where in 1930 the planet Pluto was discovered.

Flagstaff sits on the Colorado Plateau at the foot of the San Francisco Peaks and has the honor of being the highest point on all of Route 66. Highway 66 through town is home to many historic structures, including the Museum Club, a well-known roadhouse built in 1931. Listed on the National Register of Historic Places in 1994, the Museum Club continues to attract tourists with its vintage atmosphere.

West on Route 66 past the Museum Club is Flagstaff's "Motel Row." Many fine examples of 1930s and 1940s motels line this strip, albeit in varying states of repair. In 1968 Interstate 40 replaced Route 66 through Flagstaff, making it the first city in Arizona to be bypassed. In fact, it would be a full decade before another Arizona Route 66 town was bypassed.

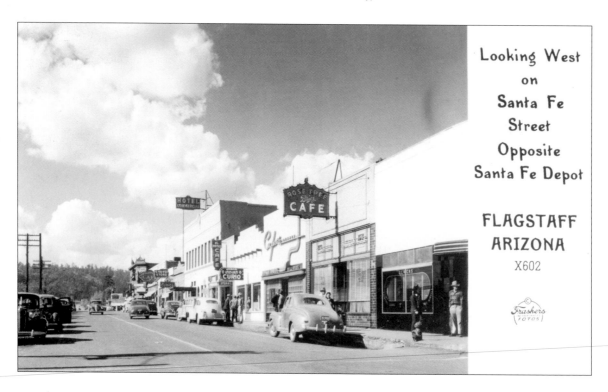

Looking West on Santa Fe Street Opposite Santa Fe Depot

FLAGSTAFF ARIZONA

X602

EL PUEBLO MOTOR INN, FLAGSTAFF
c. 1940

E. B. Goble, a local contractor, built the El Pueblo Motor Inn for Philip Johnston in 1936. Born in 1892, Johnston was the son of a Navajo missionary and is best known as the man responsible for developing the Navajo "Code Talkers" program during World War II. Growing up on the reservation as a child, he learned to speak fluent Navajo, and the complex code he developed based on this unwritten language stumped the Japanese throughout the war and saved countless American lives.

The El Pueblo Motor Inn is located 3 miles east of downtown Flagstaff "in the heart of the Old West," as proclaimed on the back of an advertising postcard. The area was considered "out in the country" when the motel was built. The El Pueblo was quite successful in its day, due in no small part to the fact that it was one of the first auto courts travelers came across when approaching the city from the east. The rooms were set back from the road in a beautiful wooded area dense with pine trees. It didn't hurt that picturesque mountains formed the backdrop. "Modern comfort in the pines" and "your home away from home" were a couple of the advertising catch phrases Johnston used to attract passing motorists.

Johnston died in 1978, but his El Pueblo Motor Inn still stands among the pines today. Granted, time, the elements, and a string of neglectful owners have taken a toll on the landmark motel. A couple of the rooms continue to be rented on a nightly basis, but most units are currently utilized as monthly rental apartments. Nevertheless, the El Pueblo Motor Inn remains a prime example of the classic 1930s-era motor court.

EL PUEBLO MOTOR INN "IN THE HEART OF THE OLD WEST" ON US HIGHWAY

PARKS IN THE PINES
GENERAL STORE, PARKS
c. 1929

The town of Parks was originally known as Rhodes, but its name was changed to Maine in 1898 in honor of the famous battleship sunk in Havana Harbor that year. Realizing there was another town in the territory called Maine, the U.S. Postal Service forced the town to find a new name. As it happened, a man by the name of Parks operated a general store and early post office in town, and it was agreed to change the name of the town to Parks in honor of this pioneer shopkeeper.

The original town site was located 2 miles east of its present location, but was moved when the first highway came through. By 1921 the Old Trails Highway was completed and quickly became well traveled as the numbers of automobile tourists grew. Soon there was a need for a good road to the Grand Canyon. Flagstaff and Williams fought over the right to have the new road begin in their town. It was deemed fair to split the difference, and the road was built from Parks. This new road was completed in June 1921.

In November of that same year, Art Anderson and Don McMillan, filling a growing need to serve these masses of tourists, built a general store and gas station at the intersection of the Old Trails Highway and the new road to the Grand Canyon. The original historic building still stands and houses a store and post office. The Flagstaff

Chamber of Commerce built the stone columns and sign over the road around the same time as the opening of the store in 1921.

In 1926 the Old Trails Highway was designated Highway 66. In 1928 flamboyant promoter C. C. Pyle (also known as "Cash and Carry" Pyle) organized a footrace to promote the new highway. Billed as "C. C. Pyle's 1st Annual International Trans-Continental Footrace," the contest became more affectionately known as the Bunion Derby. The race began March 4 at Ascot Speedway in Los Angeles and followed Highway 66 to Chicago before continuing to Madison Square Garden in New York City. The athletes ran an average of 40 miles a day through municipalities Pyle could convince to pay a fee. Andy Payne, a farm boy from Oklahoma, won, reaching New York on March 26 and claiming the $25,000 prize. Payne (No. 43) is shown at right passing the Parks in the Pines General Store.

Very little has changed about the building since the store's opening in 1921. The old wood floor strains and creaks with every step, the vintage furnishings hide tales of bygone eras, and the post office inside recalls an earlier time. In 2000 Ron and Millie Gillpatrick purchased the Parks store and continue its fine tradition of serving delicious homemade sandwiches to locals and travelers alike.

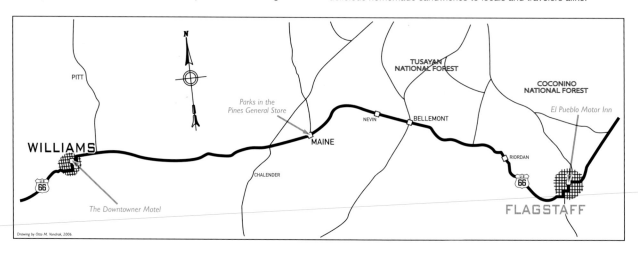

Drawing by Otto M. Vondrak, 2006.

THE DOWNTOWNER MOTEL, WILLIAMS
c. 1952

Built during the tourist explosion of the early 1950s, the Downtowner Motel remains a fine example of the modern-styled tourist motels of the era and utilizes the classic U-shaped design. Unfortunately for the owners, the U shape of the motel was doomed from the start. With the massive increase in automobile travel, Williams was overloaded with traffic. Sometime in the mid-1950s, engineers decided to split east and west traffic through town into two one-way streets. Bill Williams Avenue would carry eastbound traffic, while Railroad Avenue would carry westbound travelers.

This split created a logistics problem for the motel and its owner: access to the Downtowner from the west was essentially eliminated. To solve the problem, a portion of the rear of the motel was removed. In its place a driveway was built to allow motel access for westbound traffic.

A part of the Best Western chain and an Automobile Association of America–recommended motel, the Downtowner was a popular stopover. In 1988, Sam Vaidya purchased the motel and initiated some much-needed maintenance. Vaidya vows to preserve the classic look and feel of his 18-unit motel. He understands the importance of Williams and its relationship to Highway 66. Williams has the distinction of being the last town along the entire route to be bypassed, a somber event that took place on October 13, 1984. That same year the Downtown District of Williams became a National Register Historic District, and in 1989 Route 66 through Williams was listed on the National Register of Historic Places.

THE DOWNTOWNER MOTEL, WILLIAMS, ARIZONA

COPPER STATE COURT, ASH FORK
c. 1939

What today is known as the Copper State Court began as a Standard Oil station and general store in 1924, two years before the main street through Ash Fork became Highway 66. Situated on the east side of the once-bustling town, the Copper State Court was the creation of Ezell and Zelma Nelson. Prior to establishing the Copper State, the Nelsons were employed at the Harvey House in Kingman, Arizona. Seeking a better life for themselves, they set out to build a business of their own. The Nelsons realized their vision in 1928, when they finished adding a 12-cottage motel to the gas station and general store. The business became known as the Copper State Modern Cottages.

The cottages are set up in the classic L shape, with the office located on the west end. Each cottage was meticulously built using white river rock held together with black mortar. The natural stone survived until it was deemed necessary to do something to attract the attention of passing motorists, at which time the exteriors of the units were painted a stark white. Not only was this gambit successful, it also gave the impression of cleanliness, which of course remains a very important virtue to potential guests.

Hardwood floors were featured throughout each of the units. Eventually the hardwood was removed from the bathrooms and replaced with concrete. Other than that, all of the original hardwood remains intact. Room size varies from unit to unit but averages 12x14 feet.

Garages were situated alongside each unit, as was the norm during that era. In fact, one of the more interesting facts about this Highway 66 icon involves these garages. When the Copper State was originally built, horse travel was still a viable mode of transportation, especially in the West, and the original garages came equipped with horse railings along the inside walls. Whether used as stalls or garages, these covered spaces protected the chosen mode of transportation from the often-harsh elements. The garages have long been enclosed and now serve as storage sheds for long-term residents.

The name of the motel was eventually changed sometime during the early 1940s to the Copper State Court to keep up with the times. During the mid-1950s the gas station was remodeled to include a living space and office. Sometime during the 1960s the station closed, the gas pumps and tanks were removed, and the canopy was razed.

Both the Copper State Court and Ash Fork have had their ups and downs. During World War II, regular stops by troop trains brought thousands of servicemen and -women through town, many of whom left a portion of their hard-earned pay in one of the local cafés or bars. The 1940s and the following years brought a deluge of vacation travelers, and the Copper State and Ash Fork hit their peak. Thousands of cars per day traveled Route 66 through town, heading west to California. Ash Fork was a beehive of activity. Sometime during the 1950s, however, the Atchison, Topeka & Santa Fe Railway moved its main line 10 miles north of town, a move that had a profoundly negative impact on the local economy. Then, in the early 1970s, a ferocious fire destroyed many of the main-street businesses. The final insult occurred in 1979 when the interstate bypassed Ash Fork, leaving many businesses, including the Copper State Court, in the proverbial dust.

Current owners George and Brenda Bannister purchased the Copper State Court in October 1989 and have kept intact much of the original charm of this classic vintage motor court. The only major overhaul, according to George, was the modernization of the ancient plumbing and fixtures. He is quick to point out that the Copper State was one of the first motels in the entire region to have indoor restrooms, a feature that made the motel an extremely attractive destination for business travelers and honeymooners. He fondly remembers one morning watching a gentleman drive past the motel over a dozen times. Every time the man got close he slowed down the car but never stopped. Finally, after about a half hour or so, he stopped, got out of his car, and closely examined the grounds and the doors to every room. It turned out the man and his wife spent their honeymoon night at the Copper State Court more than 65 years earlier. "This happens on a regular basis," says George.

George is proud to report that Route 66 travelers from all over the world have stayed at the Copper State. Seven of the 12 rooms are currently rented out on a weekly or monthly basis. Room No. 4 is the only unit equipped with a kitchenette and the only room that features a separate bedroom. The remaining five units are available for overnight stays.

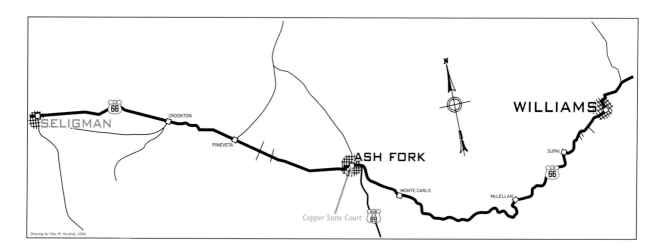

Drawing by Otto M. Vondrak, 2006

COPPER STATE COURT, ASH FORK, ARIZONA

X721

SELIGMAN
c. 1951

In the mid-1800s the area around what is today Seligman was known as Mint Valley. Settlers and pioneers traversed through the region via the Beale Wagon Road. In 1886 residents of nearby Prescott were convinced to finance a rail line called the Prescott & Arizona Central Railroad, which would connect Prescott with the Atlantic & Pacific main line via Mint Valley. With that connection, Mint Valley became known as Prescott Junction. The Prescott & Arizona Central soon went out of business, the line from Prescott Junction to Prescott was torn up, and Prescott Junction's name was changed to Seligman. It was named for two brothers who owned stock in the Atlantic & Pacific and were partners in the Aztec Land and Cattle Company.

The Atlantic & Pacific became the Atchison, Topeka & Santa Fe Railroad, or, more simply, the Santa Fe, in the late 1890s. In 1897 the Santa Fe moved its western terminus and roundhouse from Williams to Seligman, giving a huge boost to Seligman's economy. In 1905 the Santa Fe built a Harvey House dubbed El Havasu. When Highway 66 was designated in 1926, Seligman became an important stop for travelers, and once again the town reaped the benefits. Auto travel was on the rise and rail travel suffered for it. In 1954 a lack of passenger rail travel forced the Santa Fe to close the El Havasu. The building still stands and is used as office space by the BNSF Railway.

On June 29, 1956, President Dwight Eisenhower signed the Federal Highway Act, marking the beginning of the Interstate Highway System and the beginning of the end for Highway 66. On September 22, 1978, Interstate 40 bypassed Seligman. Route 66, the main street through town, suddenly fell quiet, and businesses quickly felt the effects.

Down, but not defeated, the town rallied around brothers Angel and Juan Delgadillo, who, beginning in 1985, led the current Route 66 revival and sparked new interest in the historic highway. Preaching the significance of the fabled highway to anyone who would listen, the Delgadillos were instrumental in getting the road redesignated as Historic U.S. 66. They are credited with the resurgence and increased popularity that the old road currently enjoys. Today Seligman reaps the rewards of their hard work and dedication as one of the more popular stops among tourists traveling Historic 66. A visit to the Snow Cap Drive-In, built by Juan and owned by the Delgadillo family, is a must. The drive-in is one of the most photographed and talked-about spots on all of Route 66.

7-V RANCH RESORT, VALENTINE
c. 1935

Ed Carrow began building his multipurpose ranch well before the designation of Highway 66 in 1926. Along with his six brothers, Carrow built up the business that originally consisted of a slaughterhouse and dairy to eventually include a restaurant, garage, gas station, and auto court. The 1924 restaurant on the Old Beale Road was completed from stones that he salvaged from nearby abandoned railroad bridges. The restaurant was a great success, and bus lines made the 7-V Ranch a regular meal stop. A swimming pool was later added, much to the delight of scorched bus passengers, who cooled off with a quick dip before resuming their trips.

Tourist traffic picked up after the designation of Highway 66, and Carrow built a row of eight small cabins to accommodate overnight guests. The cabins were built with two guest units in each building and sat alongside Crozier Creek, which ran through the property. Heavy rains caused the creek to flood in 1939, destroying the garage and gas station. The flood also damaged a portion of the restaurant and some of the cabins. Route 66 was soon rerouted to higher ground to avoid another disaster, thus bypassing the ranch. A few remnants of the 7-V Ranch Resort remain, including the row of cabins alongside Crozier Creek.

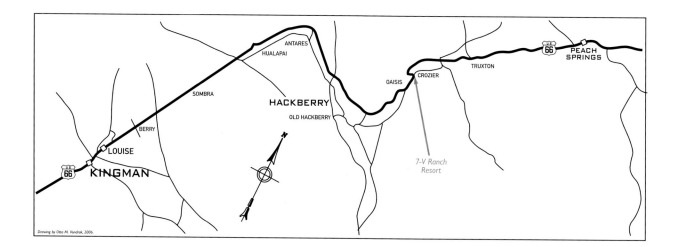

Drawing by Otto M. Vondrak, 2006.

EL TROVATORE COURT, KINGMAN
c. 1960

Since the early 1900s Kingman has served and flourished as an important transportation hub for the western United States. But when Kingman was chosen as a Highway 66 city, the tourist industry began to blossom in earnest, and dozens of auto courts sprang up along Kingman's roadside.

In the late 1930s John F. Miller purchased the future site of the El Trovatore. Miller was no stranger to the hotel business. He built his first in Las Vegas on the corner of Main and Freemont—a two-story structure later known as the Golden Gate Casino—and in December 1939 the El Trovatore received its first guests. The motel consisted of 30 units back in 1939, and overnight rates started at $3 a night. The El Trovatore became a very popular stop in Kingman, and to keep up with demand Miller added another 24 rooms. The bathrooms used hand-cut tiles in a variety of colors to add a very elegant look to each room. A cocktail lounge and dining room were also part of the facility.

The interiors of both were quite unusual, featuring walls lined with large rocks to give the impression of being inside a stone structure.

The interstate bypassed Kingman in 1953, and the El Trovatore subsequently went through a succession of ownership changes. The motel began to slowly deteriorate both in appearance and reputation. In May 2005 Karen M. Kreiger purchased the El Trovatore with plans to revitalize the motel and repair its somewhat seedy reputation. The motel is currently going through a complete renovation; the first phase was completed in 2005 and the second phase, mainly interior renovation, should be completed by April 2006. All rooms will be completely redone by then with new furniture and carpet. Although Kreiger contemplated whether to reopen the El Trovatore as an apartment complex, a motel, or a combination of both, she is leaning toward apartments because of the constant upkeep required for a motel of this size. The rear building is currently in use as monthly rentals.

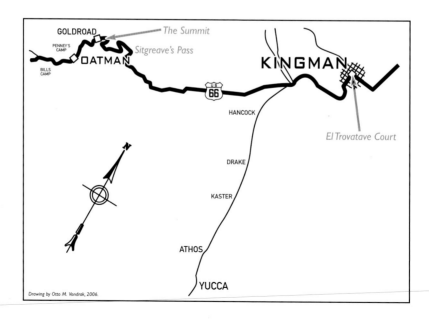

Drawing by Otto M. Vondrak, 2006.

THE SUMMIT, SITGREAVES PASS
c. 1940

As it scales the foreboding Black Mountains, Highway 66 rises to a peak of 3,550 feet above sea level between Kingman and Oatman. The pass through this mountain range was named for Captain Lorenzo Sitgreaves, who in 1851 was sent on a mission to assess the navigability of the Zuni and Colorado rivers for use in a possible confrontation with the Mormon settlement in Utah. Around 1861 Sitgreaves Pass was the site of an immigrant massacre by the Hualapi and Mohave Indians.

The Summit filling station and ice cream parlor was located 24 miles west of Kingman, on the first routing of Route 66 through the Black Mountains at the summit of Sitgreaves Pass. Imagine inching up the pass in your automobile. The car has no air conditioning, and as hot as it is outside, it is hotter in the car. The gas gauge is reading low. You should have listened to your wife and filled up earlier. The kids are complaining every step of the way. Your throats are parched. As the car struggles on, beads of sweat fall from your forehead, clouding your vision. As you reach the summit, you are just able to make out a sign ahead on the right. Does that sign say "Ice Cream"? No, it couldn't be. Ice cream and beer!? The kids see the ice cream sign and demand you pull over. Of course you were going to anyway. This scene probably occurred several times a day on this section of Route 66. The Summit must have been a strange and wonderful sight after taking on the perils of the pass.

Today memories of relieved parents and children's faces dripping with ice cream, as well as a few crumbling foundations, are all that are left of the Summit, which burned to the ground in 1967.

TOPOCK
c. 1941

Topock began in 1883 as a small settlement populated by bridge builders and railroad employees who were constructing the first bridge across this section of the Colorado River. The area was chosen for the crossing because of the narrow width of the river at this point. When a post office was established in 1906, the settlement was originally called Acme, but was later changed to Topock, a Native American word for "water crossing."

There is no real town of Topock, and to give you an idea of how little there is here, the Topock post office is actually located in the nearby community of Golden Shores. The Needles Ferry was established here in 1890 and was the only way to cross the river if you were not traveling by rail. The ferry continued to carry travelers across the Colorado until a flood destroyed the facility in 1914. *A Guidebook to Highway 66* (1946) states that Topock's facilities at that time included "gas, grocery, a few cabins and a garage for light repairs; limited facilities." Nothing remains of these "limited facilities," although there is a marina on the shores of the Colorado River.

CALIFORNIA

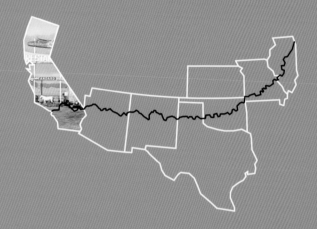

TRAILS ARCH BRIDGE
AND RED ROCK BRIDGE
c. 1933

The first bridge to cross the Colorado River at Topock was a wooden structure built by the railroad in 1883. In 1890 the Phoenix Bridge Company built one of the first steel bridges in the country, the Red Rock Bridge, to replace the outdated wooden bridge for the Atlantic & Pacific Railroad. With a construction cost of almost a half million dollars, the Red Rock Bridge was thought to be excessive and very expensive at the time. Trains quickly became heavier and stressed the limits of the new steel bridge. Modifications were needed to strengthen the structure, first in 1901, then again in 1911.

If you were not traveling by train, crossing the Colorado was a different story. Prior to the automobile, the Needles Ferry carried horse and foot traffic across the Colorado beginning in 1890. When the automobile appeared on the scene, this ferry served motor traffic traveling the Old National Trails Highway. In 1914 a massive flood took out the ferry service, leaving travelers stranded on both sides of the river. Wooden planks were laid over the railroad ties of the bridge. Motorists were allowed to cross between trains, as railroad employees with train schedules in hand coordinated the crossings.

The Red Rock Bridge continued to carry automobile traffic until the Old Trails Arch Bridge was completed on February 20, 1916. The first alignment of Route 66 crossed the Colorado River from Topock, Arizona, to Needles, California (14 miles to the west) via this bridge, seen in the background of the postcard and photograph. The Old Trails Arch Bridge carried the dirt path of the National Old Trails Highway for more than 10 years prior to the designation of U.S. Highway 66 in 1926. Located about 800 feet downstream of the Red Rock Bridge, the Old Trails Arch Bridge was a marvel in its own right. For 12 years it stood as the longest three-hinged arch bridge in the country.

Although it was quite the engineering accomplishment at the time, the bridge had its limitations. The load limit was only 11 tons,

and the roadbed was so narrow that bus and truck traffic were able to cross only one way at a time. A warning sign was posted at both ends of the bridge to help avoid head-on collisions: "One Way for Trucks and Buses." This restriction proved quite annoying to motorists from time to time, but for the most part traffic was light enough and did not pose serious problems until later years.

With the coming of World War II, truck traffic on all of America's highways increased dramatically. This increase, along with the growing size of vehicles, spelled the beginning of the end for the Old Trails Arch Bridge. Automobile travel and truck traffic continued to grow by leaps and bounds, especially in the years immediately following World War II. The graceful old bridge was no longer able to handle the heavy traffic load that Highway 66 now supported. A new automobile crossing over the Colorado was desperately needed.

In 1945 the Santa Fe Railway established a new river crossing, opening the possibility for auto traffic to once again flow over the Red Rock Bridge. It was determined that an adequate crossing was already in place and a new bridge did not need to be built. The rails and ties were removed from the Red Rock Bridge and concrete was poured for the roadbed. On May 21, 1947, the Red Rock Railroad Bridge conversion was complete, and automobile traffic once again flowed over the venerable bridge. When the new four-lane steel bridge carrying Interstate 40 was completed in 1966, the Red Rock Bridge was unceremoniously closed and remained abandoned until it was completely dismantled in 1976. Only the concrete pilings remain.

The Old Trails Arch Bridge, once in danger of the same fate, was again put to use and today carries a natural gas pipeline from Texas for the Pacific Gas and Electric Company. For a nice look at the Old Trails Arch Bridge in its heyday, watch the Joads cross it in the movie version of John Steinbeck's novel *The Grapes of Wrath*.

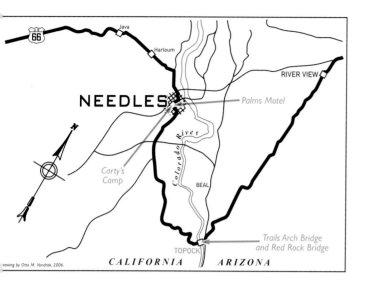

TOPOC AND SANTA FE RAILWAY BRIDGES OVER COLORADO RIVER, NEAR NEEDLES, CAL.

CARTY'S CAMP, NEEDLES
c. 1931

While visiting the Grand Canyon, Santa Fe Railway employee Bill Carty stayed in a cabin that was something of a tent/cabin hybrid. Upon his return to Needles, he enthusiastically brought up the idea of starting a tourist camp and auto court to a friend and coworker, one Mr. Manskar. Manskar thought it was a great idea to open an auto camp in Needles, and in 1925 Carty's Camp became a reality. Both the Carty and Manskar families were involved in operating the facility, and both lived on the premises for a time. Manskar grew weary of the business, though, and Carty eventually bought out his interest. Carty quit his position at the railroad to manage the business full time.

The facility eventually expanded to include a gas station, garage, cottages, campground, and a motel, which Carty dubbed Havasu Court. Havasu Court consisted of 12 cabins, each with an attached garage, in two back-to-back rows. Shade in Needles is gold, especially in the summer months when temperatures can climb into the high 120s, and a small, shaded picnic area located directly across from the camp was a favorite among customers. Carty's Camp flourished and became the place to stay in Needles.

Carty retired from the business in 1948 and sold the camp to Charles Canterbury and Loren Armes. Both the Canterbury and Armes families shared the day-to-day operations, and, like their predecessors, both families lived on-site. Mildred Armes remembers Route 66 as a gold mine that provided customers from 6 a.m. to 10 p.m. every day. "We worked our tails off," she was quoted as saying. The two families also built and operated a gas station in Needles called the C&A Chevron Gas Station, which included a lunchroom and store. Eventually the families retired from the business, and the camp closed shortly thereafter. Not much is left of the remaining structures, on which the desert climate has taken its toll. Today a few of the cabins are used for storage.

Carty's Camp was a true reflection of what auto travel on early Highway 66 was all about. The Joad family passed in front of Carty's in the screen version of *The Grapes of Wrath*. That appearance in itself makes the site of Carty's Camp hallowed grounds. Just standing on the property, one hearkens back to the days of early auto travel when excitement, adventure, and even danger were part of an automobile trip. That real sense of adventure is captured on a note written on the back of a postcard dated June 24, 1931: "Dear Daddie, It is now 11:55 p.m. We are going on across the desert tonight. It is very hot and dry. We will write when we get on the other side. Love Florence."

THE PALMS MOTEL, NEEDLES
c. 1946

Needles was always an important stop along Highway 66. For westbound travelers, it was the jumping-off point for crossing the treacherous Mojave. Those headed east and emerging from the Mojave took a deep breath, gave a sigh of relief, and thanked their lucky stars to have made it without incident.

The Palms Motel is located on the eastern edge of town where Broadway and Front Street split. The motel's origins date to the 1920s, when it was located on the west edge of town. In the motel business they say location is everything, and the cabins were eventually moved to their current location in the late 1930s. Prior to the move, the eastern location was the site of a tent camp for the railroad, and the Palms soon became a favorite sleepover for railroad employees.

Along with Carty's Camp, the Palms Motel was one of the first tourist facilities that weary westbound travelers saw when approaching Needles. Operated by Guy and Orsavella Austin in its early days, it consisted of 14 units, 8 of which had kitchen facilities.

The Palms has gone through a succession of owners. In 1991 Hank and Edna Wilde purchased the property from Luis Bravo and transformed the motel into a bed and breakfast renamed the Old Trails Inn. The B&B never really took off, and it closed in 1997. Bravo reacquired the property and proceeded to fully renovate each unit. The walls were stripped bare, and new plumbing and wiring were installed throughout the property. The Palms currently has 16 units, all of which are rented monthly.

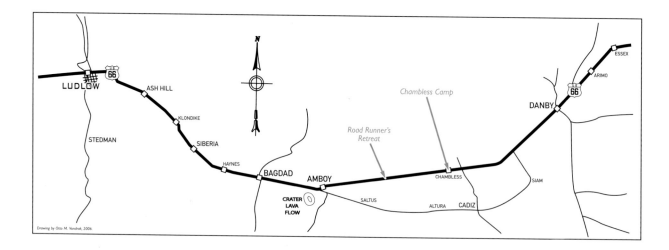

Drawing by Otto M. Vondrak, 2006.

CHAMBLESS CAMP, CHAMBLESS
c. 1932

In the 1920s a widower named James A. Chambless, along with his two children, relocated from Arkansas to the Amboy, California, area. In 1932 he built the small Chambless Camp out of handmade blocks, hoping to cash in on the burgeoning auto-tourist trade. He quickly expanded the business into a full-service stop that included a service station, café, grocery, and cabins. The main building, housing the grocery and service station, featured a large canopy over the pumps to provide shade to customers while they were filling up. Jack D. Rittenhouse, in his 1946 book, *A Guidebook to Highway 66*, describes the Chambless Camp as "one of the few shady spots in the entire desert route."

Much of the business relied on first-time desert travelers who unknowingly attempted to cross the desert during the heat of the day. Wreckers were at the ready, mechanics were on duty, the café was open to feed stranded travelers, and cabins were available for overnight stays if repairs were extensive. Sometime in the late 1930s, Chambless was remarried to a woman named Fannie Gould.

She took over the reins of the business and turned the Chambless Camp into a virtual desert oasis, adding, among other things, a fishpond and a sprawling rose garden, both very unusual sights in this region of the Mojave Desert. In addition, a picnic area lined with acacia trees provided shade and added the oasis-like feel of the grounds.

The early 1970s saw the opening of Interstate 40, and most businesses along this stretch of Highway 66 soon closed. Sometime in the early 1990s, the canopy over the gasoline pumps at the Chambless Camp was destroyed in a violent windstorm, and more recently the pumps were removed. Gus Lizalde bought the property in the early 1990s and planned to renovate the camp to include a Mexican restaurant, a remodeled service station, and RV hookups. The restaurant was open for a time, but the rest of the renovations never really got off the ground. The old cabins still stand and are rented to workers who farm the vineyards in nearby Cadiz. The majority of the property remains abandoned and is, inch by inch, being slowly reclaimed by the harsh desert elements.

ROAD RUNNER'S RETREAT, EAST AMBOY
c. 1960

Located 9 miles east of Amboy and a short half mile west of the Chambless Camp, the Road Runner's Retreat was a relative latecomer along Route 66 in this part of the Mojave, opening sometime in the mid- to late 1950s. The restaurant served classic road food and was an extremely popular stop for truckers. The interstate bypassed this section of Highway 66 in the early 1970s, leaving most of the businesses from Essex to Ludlow, including the Road Runner's Retreat, high and dry.

In 1988 the Road Runner's Retreat received a face-lift when Dodge decided to film a television commercial on the site. For a couple of days the gas station and restaurant once again jumped with the hustle and bustle of people coming and going. The clamor of cars pulling in and out of the gas station and restaurant must have truly been a strange sight for the local wildlife. Then, just as suddenly as the silence was broken, order was restored, and the wild creatures and birds reinhabited the empty structures. It is stunning how loud the quiet is here and how much of an outsider humans truly are. As a light breeze breaks the silence and makes its way through the hollow buildings, perhaps a faint sound, barely audible, can be heard— maybe it's a friendly "Beep beep."

CALIFORNIA AGRICULTURAL INSPECTION STATION, DAGGETT
c. 1953

This California Agricultural Inspection Station was built in 1953 and was the third of three such stations built in Daggett. Agricultural inspection stations were set up all around California in an effort to prevent the import and transport of diseased fruits and plants and harmful parasites. These searches prevented fast-moving diseases and parasites from devastating entire crops and so protected the state's large, important citrus and vegetable industries. All westbound traffic was stopped, and each car was given a complete and thorough search. Plants, fruits, and vegetables were quickly confiscated, and incoming motorists were then given an inspection and admission certificate allowing them to pass.

Interstate 40 eventually replaced Route 66 in the area, and the Daggett station was permanently shut down in 1967. (The current inspection station sits on the super slab just outside of Needles.) The second of the three inspection stations was built in 1930 and is the one seen in the 1940 movie version of *The Grapes of Wrath*. Sadly, during the 1930s, these inspection stations and dozens of makeshift stations around the state were often used to weed out "undesirables" as thousands fled the choking, dust-ridden plains of the Midwest. Thousands of people were turned away when inspectors deemed them unfit to pass. It is said that many of these displaced Okies and Arkies, without the means to satisfy inspectors—and virtually stripped of all hope for a future—walked despondently into the desert, never to be seen again.

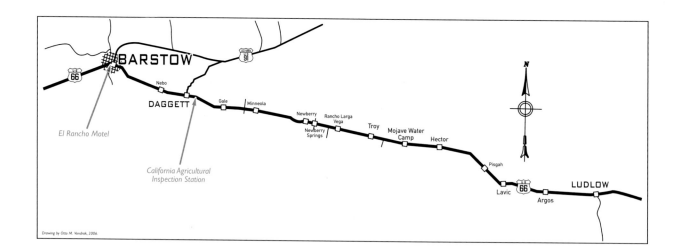

EL RANCHO MOTEL, BARSTOW
c. 1947

A man named Cliff Chase built the El Rancho Motel in 1947 entirely from old railroad ties salvaged from the Tonopah & Tidewater Railroad. During the heyday of Route 66, Barstow became an essential stop for travelers arriving from the tough Mojave portion of the road or preparing themselves for the dreaded desert journey. The El Rancho provided excellent facilities, and the motel was regularly filled to capacity. Originally the El Rancho contained 50 rooms, but at its peak it featured 101 rooms, 26 of them with kitchenettes. In 1947 room rates started at $4.50 a night for a single bed and went up from there. A 100-foot-tall neon sign later erected on the property became a beacon that could be seen for miles.

In 1979 the motel was closed to the public and rented exclusively by the Santa Fe Railway and its employees. When Interstates 15 and 40 were completed, newer and more convenient motels were built alongside the new highways, and the El Rancho slowly fell into disrepair. In 1987 Rick Byers bought the property and began the process of restoration. It was reopened only to close five years later, again deteriorating due to hard times and poor management. In 1994 Byers sank another $300,000 into a second restoration, which included a Route 66 Visitor's Center adjacent to the motel office. Unfortunately, current traffic on Historic Route 66 did not generate sufficient business to justify keeping the motel well maintained, and once again the motel is headed on a downward slide. Surviving several subsequent ownership changes, the El Rancho continues to operate as a senior housing facility. Willing motorists can still spend the night at the vintage motel, as several rooms have been set aside to accommodate the courageous and weary tourist.

The
EL RANCHO
MOTEL

at
BARSTOW,
California

at the
junction of
U. S. Highways
466, 91 and 66

F6655

GREEN SPOT MOTEL, VICTORVILLE
c. 1947

Heading west through Victorville, the path of Highway 66 ran down D Street until reaching Seventh Street, where the Mother Road took a rare 90-degree turn and continued on through town. One block after the turn, near the corner of Seventh and C Streets, sits the landmark Green Spot Motel. In its heyday Victorville served as backdrop for hundreds of Hollywood Westerns and as a getaway for the stars. The Green Spot Motel was the crème de la crème. The motel consisted of 20 gable-roofed buildings, each containing two guest units with flat-roofed carports connecting them. The buildings were arranged in a U shape with 10 across the rear and 5 along each side. In the center was a magnificently landscaped courtyard that later contained a swimming pool.

The Green Spot was at one time part of the United Auto Courts system and billed as "Truly De Luxe." A café, also called the Green Spot, was located on the corner of C Street and Seventh. Very popular in its day, the café was frequented by many a celebrity. Orson Welles was rumored to have written much of his material in one of the booths. In 1953 the Green Spot Café burned to the ground.

After the interstate bypass was built in 1972, the motel began the typical decline and soon became home to drug dealing and prostitution. In 1982, the 1940s star Kay Aldridge, best known for her portrayal of Nyoka in the serial *Perils of Nyoka*, married Harry Nasland, who was then part owner of the Green Spot Motel. He died after a few months of marriage, and Aldridge inherited his interest in the motel. She vowed to clean up the place and restore it to its original splendor as a premier getaway and rest stop. It was more than she could handle. She eventually became disillusioned and moved to Maine. A plaque located on the front wall next to the entrance arch reads "Nyoka's Hideaway," bearing witness to her fondness for the Green Spot.

Aldridge sold the motel to Benjamin Wu and Nancy Wei, who operated it until 1995. Aldridge died of a heart attack on January 12, 1995, and two months later Wei was sentenced to 13 years in prison for shooting and killing her husband. Aldridge's estate foreclosed on the property, and the Green Spot sat dormant. It was eventually sold to Hemant Patel in 2001. The Green Spot Motel currently rents to weekly and monthly tenants and is showing signs of a slight recovery.

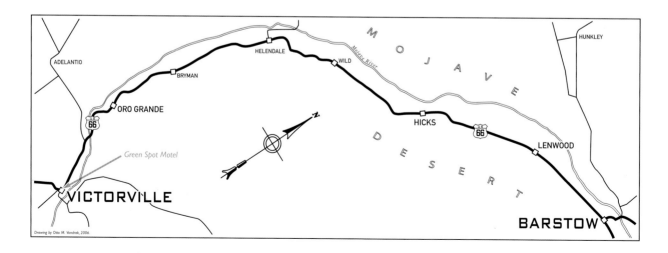

Drawing by Otto M. Vondrak, 2006.

SUMMIT INN, CAJON SUMMIT
c. 1957

The Summit Inn was built in 1952 by Burton and Dorothy Riley on what was then two-lane Route 66. The roadbed sat on the east side of the restaurant at the time of the hotel's construction, but was moved in 1955 to its current location on the west side when it was upgraded to four-lane status. The restaurant sat on the west side of the road when C. A. Stevens purchased the business from the Rileys on October 13, 1966. Stevens has owned and operated it ever since.

In 1969 and 1970, Interstate 15 obliterated the Mother Road in this area, but the Summit Inn survived the changes and continues to serve good road fare. In 1969 Stevens moved the service station end of the business closer to the off-ramp that was being built as part of the new interstate upgrade. As late as 1972, water had to be hauled to the Summit Inn by truck and was pumped into the restaurant from a storage tank located alongside the restaurant.

When Stevens bought the business, he also acquired a waitress by the name of Hilda Fish, who continued working at the Summit Inn until retirement in 2002. During the late 1980s, representatives of the Denny's Corporation approached Stevens with an offer to convert the restaurant. When Stevens asked Fish what she thought of the idea, she responded, "You put a Denny's here and I quit." The Denny's was never built, and Fish stayed.

The Summit Inn continues to be a popular stop on the Cajon Pass—so popular that even the King himself, Elvis Presley, was reported to have paid a visit. According to Fish, Elvis stopped at the Summit Inn one night, but left hurriedly when he saw that none of his records were in the jukebox. It's true—Elvis *has* left the building.

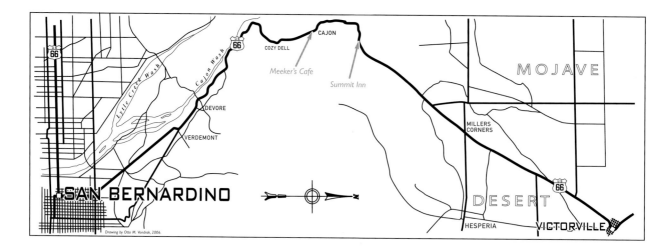

MEEKER'S CAFÉ, CAJON PASS
c. 1932

The path over and through the Cajon Pass has gone through several forms and variations. Early on it was a narrow, difficult-to-navigate pack trail known as the Spanish Trail. By 1855 the trail was moved farther east, and although improved, it added several miles to the trip. In 1861, with financial backing from Henry M. Willis and George L. Tucker, John Brown built a new road for which he would charge a toll of 25 cents for a man and his horse and $1 for a horse-driven wagon. As time went on, the path through the pass evolved and has been known as Old Trails Highway, Highway 66, and, currently, Interstate 15.

In 1919 Marion Meeker built a small gas station and café on leased land next to Camp Cajon on what was then Old Trails Highway. Built by William Marion Bristol, Camp Cajon was a rest stop and picnic area that acted as a welcome station at the "Gateway to Southern California." Meeker's brother, Ezra, soon arrived to lend a hand. By 1929 the brothers had saved enough money to buy their own land, and they built a new place just down the road. They soon had their gas station, café, and store up and running, along with an auto court called Meeker's Sunrise Cabins.

The year 1946 saw the complete destruction of the café and garage by a runaway truck that luckily missed the gasoline pumps. In the mid-1950s the whole complex was torn down to make room for the new four-lane Route 66. Only two cabins survived, and they were relocated, combined, and converted into a small house. A new garage, café, and gas station were built on the remaining property. Ezra ran the place until his death in 1966. His second wife, Mabel, who was also known as the "Angel of Cajon Pass," lived in the converted house until 2002, when she moved to a senior-care facility.

The Cajon Pass has a wonderfully rich history that can be traced back well over 150 years. Although little remains of Camp Cajon and Meeker's Café, the pathway through the pass continues to be a vital transportation corridor to this day.

FIGUEROA STREET TUNNELS/ARROYO SECO PARKWAY, LOS ANGELES
c. 1943

Construction of three of the four Figueroa Street Tunnels was completed in 1931, and the fourth and final tunnel was completed in 1936. That same year saw Route 66 rerouted through the tunnels. The downtown Los Angeles terminus at Broadway and Seventh changed to Olympic and Lincoln Boulevard in Santa Monica and was reached via Sunset Boulevard and Santa Monica Boulevard.

Construction of the Arroyo Seco Parkway, extending from Pasadena en route to Los Angeles, began in 1938. December 30, 1940, saw the completion and opening of the beautiful, groundbreaking parkway. This Highway 66 bypass alignment was considered to be the first freeway west of the Mississippi. In 1942 two-way traffic through the Figueroa Tunnels was altered to handle one-way, northbound traffic, and the Arroyo Seco Parkway/Route 66 was extended toward downtown Los Angeles to include the Figueroa Street Tunnels.

Today, although Arroyo Seco Parkway is a beautiful drive, safety is a big concern. When dedicated, parkway speeds were set at a maximum of 45 miles per hour. With tight curves, narrow lanes, lack of shoulder space, and very little room for entering and exiting, traveling at today's speeds makes navigating the parkway somewhat challenging. It is now listed as a National Scenic Byway and is well worth the effort to explore its historic path.

AFTERWORD

For fans and devotees of the Mother Road, nothing tugs at the heartstrings or elicits more emotion than the loss of a favorite roadside stop. What we sometimes forget but should keep in mind is that from the day Highway 66 was designated as an official U.S. highway, it has undergone change and transformation. Countless motels, cafés, and service stations, many of which we will never know, have been built and destroyed from the highway's beginning. Whole towns have been bypassed, dangerous curves have been straightened, and the road's pathway has been rerouted hundreds of times. Someone's favorite eatery or service station somewhere along the road was always disappearing.

Route 66 connected the fabric of our society with a 2,400-mile concrete ribbon woven through small towns, cities, mountains, and deserts. When we changed, the road changed. The road and roadside culture became a reflection of the times. Even today, the road continues to evolve, transforming the landscape of our favorite highway, which continues to be a reflection of who we are and a mirror of our times. You may not like the changes, but we are still in that reflection just the same.

Someone once said that Route 66 meant going somewhere. It did and still does. It also meant change. Change is inevitable, and even an old, beloved historic highway goes through its share. Sometimes it is a quick transformation and other times it is a slow decay. Several places that I covered in the first *Route 66 Lost & Found* (2004) have since undergone significant changes. Some were lost. I sincerely hope none of your favorites was among them. Here is an update.

Zora Vidas, the owner of the **Wishing Well Motel**, passed away in 2004. As a result, the La Grange, Illinois, motel was sold and its doors closed for good in June 2005. At this writing, the 64-year-old motel was slated to be razed to make way for a modern condominium complex. Luckily, due to efforts by the Illinois Route 66 Preservation Foundation, the motel's sign and its unique stone well will be spared. Vidas was a special lady, and the Wishing Well Motel was a very special place, indeed. Both will be missed by many.

Pages 310 and 311: Wishing Well Motel, c.1946

The **Winona Trading Post** has existed on Route 66 in one form or another since the 1920s, and it has been at its current location since a rerouting of the highway in the early 1950s. Thankfully, it is still there, albeit with a new and different look. Since the early 1950s, bright Texaco red was prominent on the service station signage. What a visual shock it was to drive by and see the bright yellow of Shell displayed after all these years. Although it is merely a cosmetic change, it will take some getting used to.

The **Log Cabin Lodge** in Gallup, New Mexico, was not as lucky as the Winona Trading Post. The once-popular overnight stop underwent a painful decline that began in earnest in the early 1990s. Lovingly built in 1937 by Tony and Francis Leon, the Log Cabin Lodge served travelers on Route 66 for more than 60 years. Early on dubbed Log Cabin Camp, it was a one-of-a-kind auto court originally consisting of six individual log cabins, each containing a stone fireplace. The log cabins were the perfect setting for an overnight stay out West and undoubtedly fulfilled every kid's cowboy fantasy of the perfect hideout.

The Log Cabin Lodge was listed on the National Register of Historic Places in 1993, but that was not enough to forestall the inevitable. The lodge served its last guest in the mid-1990s and subsequently began its slide into a terminal state of disrepair, becoming home to transients, drug dealers, and worse. The estimated cost for restoration was in the millions and well beyond what most investors considered viable. Deemed an eyesore by most citizens of Gallup, it was ordered condemned without hesitation. On May 14, 2004, one of the most distinctive overnight stays along the entire route was razed.

Log Cabin Lodge, c.1952

Log Cabin Lodge, c. 2003

AFTERWORD

My interview in 2003 with the manager of the **Shady Rest Court**, Lori Murphy, was upbeat and positive in regard to the future of the inn. Murphy stated that small but positive steps were being taken to bring the old West Tulsa, Oklahoma, motor court back to life. In the photo taken in 2003, you can see these improvements being made. Plans were also under way to restore the vintage neon sign. This renovation did not last long, however, and once again the Shady Rest was on a fast track to an irreparable state. The story is an all too familiar one of a vintage Route 66 motel—a onetime safe haven for travelers—turned into a seedy flophouse. In late 2005 the local health department pulled the plug on the venerable old motor court. A few weeks later Shady Rest was bulldozed and reduced to a pile of rubble. Built by Maurice Colpitts in 1936, the Shady Rest Court served motorists for decades. In a way, it's nice to see the old Shady Rest taken out of its miserable state and put to rest. Colpitts, I am sure, would heartily agree.

Below: Log Cabin Lodge, c. 2003

Cool Springs Camp near Kingman, Arizona, had been closed, mostly forgotten, and ignored since 1966. Vandals slowly destroyed it, and what they did not destroy crumbled and decayed in the unforgiving heat of the desert. For one day in 1991, Cool Springs came to life as a set in the movie *Universal Soldier*. Unfortunately, it was only rebuilt for one purpose: to be blown up for a scene in the movie. The studio eventually moved on, and what they left of Cool Springs was not worth mentioning. There it sat again, a skeleton of what was once a favorite Route 66 roadside eatery among tourists and locals alike.

In 1997 a man named Ned Leuchtner happened to pass through the area and noticed the sparse ruins of Cool Springs. He decided to stop and take a look. The more he dug up, the more he became fascinated with Cool Springs and its colorful history. Researching Cool Springs Camp was fulfilling, but rebuilding the roadside icon became Leuchtner's dream and goal. He contacted a local real estate broker in Kingman to locate the owners of the property.

He contacted Nancy Waverka, the niece of prior owner Floyd Spidell, and made a few offers, but Waverka refused each, citing sentimental reasons. Leuchtner assured her that he intended to rebuild the camp and eventually gave Waverka the peace of mind she needed to sell. In the summer of 2001, Leuchtner became the overjoyed owner of Cool Springs Camp.

In the fall of 2004, the rebuilding began in earnest. Leuchtner teamed up with general contractor Dennis De Chenne. On December 7, after almost 40 years of darkness, power was hooked up and once again the lights of the Cool Springs Camp lit the night sky. The construction continues. A museum has been proposed where the one-time café building stood, and expansion of the existing gift shop is planned. Although there will be no food service or gasoline, snacks and soft drinks will be sold. With the combined efforts of Leuchtner; site manager De Chenne; and gift-shop manager Betsy Miller and her staff, Judy De Chenne and Lois Cummiskey, the spirit of Cool Springs Camp lives on.

Cool Springs Camp, 2004

Sources

Books

Curtis, C. H. *The Missouri US 66 Tour Book*. St. Louis, Mo.: D. I. Enterprises, 1994.

Graham, Shellee. *Tales from the Coral Court: Photos & Stories from a Lost Route 66 Landmark*. St. Louis, Mo.: Virginia Publishing, 2000.

Noe, Sally. *66 Sights on Route 66*. Gallup, N.M.: Gallup Downtown Development Group, 1992.

Piotrowski, Scott. *Finding the End of the Mother Road*. Pasadena, Calif.: 66 Productions, 2003.

Repp, Thomas Arthur. *Route 66: The Empires of Amusement*. Lynwood, Wash.: Mock Turtle Press, 1999.

———. *Route 66: The Romance of the West*. Lynwood, Wash.: Mock Turtle Press, 2002.

Rittenhouse, Jack D. *A Guide Book to Highway 66*. Albuquerque, N.M.: (Reprint of 1946 printing) Univ. of New Mexico Press, 1989.

Ross, Jim. *Oklahoma Route 66*. Arcadia, Okla. Ghost Town Press, 2001.

Schneider, Jill. *Route 66 Across New Mexico: A Wanderer's Guide*. Albuquerque, N.M.: Univ. of New Mexico Press, 1991.

Scott, Quinta and Susan Croce Kelly. *Route 66: The Highway and Its People*. Norman, Okla.: Univ. of Oklahoma Press, 1988.

———. *Along Route 66*. Norman, Okla.: Univ. of Oklahoma Press, 2000.

Snyder, Tom. *The Route 66 Traveler's Companion*. New York: St. Martin's Press, 1990.

Teague, Thomas. *Searching for 66*. Springfield, Ill.: Samizdat House, 1991.

Wallis, Michael. *Route 66: The Mother Road*. New York: St. Martin's Press, 1990.

Weis, John. *Traveling the New, Historic Route 66 of Illinois*. Frankfort, Ill.: A. O. Motivation Programs, 1997.

Witzel, Michael. *Route 66 Remembered*. Osceola, Wis.: Motorbooks International, 1996.

Periodicals

National Historic Route 66 Federation News (www.national66.org), 1995–2006.

Route 66 Magazine (www.route66magazine.com), 1993–2006.

Wallace, Norman. "The Scenic Wonderland Highway." *Arizona Highways* May 1955

Interviews

Adam, Nick. Ariston Café, Litchfield, Ill.
Alderson, Jace. Sands Motel, Moriarty, N.M.
Bannister, George. Copper State Court, Ash Fork, Ariz.
Berger, Lois. Log Cabin Lodge, Gallup, N.M.
Brace, Frank and Susan. Arcadia Lodge, Kingman, Ariz.
Bravo, Luis. Palms Motel, Needles, Calif.
Delgadillo, Robert. Snow Cap, Seligman, Ariz.
Edmunds, Dub. Jesse's Café/MidPoint Café, Adrian, Tex.
Edwards, Ernie. Ernie's Pig Hip, Broadwell, Ill.
Ferguson, John. Boots Motel, Carthage, Mo.
Goodridge, Edward. Vernelle's Motel, Newburg, Mo.
Hauser, Fran. MidPoint Café, Adrian, Tex.
Kraft, Bob. The Riviera, Gardner, Ill.
Krieger, Karen. El Trovatore, Kingman, Ariz.
Lehman, Ramona. Munger-Moss Motel, Lebanon, Mo.
Manker, Gina. Log Cabin Inn, Pontiac, Ill.
McPherson, Olind. Rut's Corner Café, Litchfield, Ill.
Miller, Atholl "Jiggs". Devils Elbow, Mo.
Mudd, Roy. Wagon Wheel Motel, Cuba, Mo.
Murphy, Lorie. Shady Rest Court, West Tulsa, Okla.
Natha, Mohamed. Aztec Motel, Albuquerque, N.M.
Noe, Sally. Thoreau, N.M.
Patel, Jack. Desert Hills Motel, Tulsa, Okla.
Patel, Suresh. Luna Lodge, Albuquerque, N.M.
Pendya, Mr. Rest Haven Motor Court, Springfield, Mo.
Radosevich, John. Johnnie's Café, Thoreau, N.M.
Rhea, Patrick. Del Rhea's Chicken Basket, Willowbrook, Ill.
Roberts, Teresa. Pioneer Motel, Springfield, Ill.
Sanchez Jr., Canuto. Lakeview Courts, Santa Rosa, N.M.
Stevens, C. A. Summit Inn, Cajon Pass, Calif.
Stevens, Les. Steve's Café, Chenoa, Ill.
Vaidya, San. Downtowner Motel, Williams, Ariz.
Vidas, Zora. Wishing Well Motel, LaGrange, Ill.
Waldmire, Sue. Cozy Dog, Springfield, Ill.
Werth, Wilfred. Redwood Motel, Lincoln, Ill.
Whaley, Tresa. Vega Motel, Vega, Tex.
Wheatley, Betty. Avon Courts/Buffalo Ranch, Afton, Okla.
Young, Alan. Luna Café, Mitchell, Ill.

INDEX